BLACK COUNTRY GHOSTS AND HAUNTINGS

Black Country Ghosts and Hauntings

A Gazetteer Guide

ANDREW HOMER

Tin Typewriter Publishing

Copyright © 2017 Andrew Homer

First published 2017
Tin Typewriter Publishing
Sedgley
www.tintypewriter.com

All rights reserved.

ISBN: 1540388689
ISBN-13: 978-1540388681

Cover picture White Ladies Priory

CONTENTS

About the author	6	Oldswinford	75
Acknowledgements	7	Penn	77
Introduction	9	Sedgley	79
		Shropshire (east)	85
Bilston	12	Smethwick	94
Bloxwich	17	Stourbridge	99
Brierley Hill	20	Tettenhall	108
Colley Gate	21	Tipton	110
Coseley	22	Trysull	114
Cradley Heath	24	Wall Heath	117
Darlaston	25	Walsall	118
Dudley	26	Wednesbury	128
Enville	47	West Bromwich	133
Gornal	48	Willenhall	141
Hagley	56	Wollaston	146
Halesowen	57	Wolverhampton	147
Himley	60	Wombourne	166
Kinver	66	Wordsley	168
Netherton	72		
Oldbury	73	*Bibliography*	171

ABOUT THE AUTHOR

Andrew Homer has written extensively on the Black Country and Shropshire. His previous books include *Beer and Spirits*, *Haunted Hostelries of Shropshire* and *A Black Country Miscellany*. He has presented lectures to a range of organisations over the years and appeared on local and national television. After a career as a College Lecturer Andrew now works as a Costumed Demonstrator at the Black Country Living Museum and can be found explaining the history of the buildings and the stories of the people who helped forge the Black Country. When not involved in working or writing Andrew enjoys investigating and collecting local ghost stories, particularly those which have historical connections.

ACKNOWLEDGMENTS

I am very grateful to all the people who helped out in any way. In particular, Nick Williamson who collaborated on the earlier GhostNav Black Country Ghosts project and Sophie Homer who provided original artwork. Nick Duffy and the West Midlands Ghost Club together with Lynnette Sharratt and Smethwick Paranormal Investigators for providing local stories. I'm also grateful to Janene Hall, Ann Key, Claire Dolman and Keith Hodgkins for their contributions and Chris Cooper for stories collected by Brian Perry.

Additional photography was supplied by Steve Potter, Dave Marsh, Tony Cowell and the late Alan Price. Thanks are also due to the 'Lost Pubs Project' and 'The History of Wednesbury'. Halesowen Abbey by Gordon Griffiths is reproduced under a Creative Commons Licence together with Oldswinford Cross by P. L. Chadwick, Sandwell Priory by Sjwells53 and Victorian New Street Station. The vast majority of images are from Andrew Homer's own personal collection and where not every effort has been made to ascertain copyright ownership. Any due acknowledgement which has been inadvertently omitted or any unintentional infringement of copyright will be corrected in future copies of this work.

INTRODUCTION

Black Country Ghosts and Hauntings is a ghostly gazetteer guide to over 150 spooky locations from in and around this area of the West Midlands. The Black Country has never been a clearly defined area and so whilst most of these haunted locations are most definitely 'Black Country' also included are some ghostly tales from a little further afield such as the haunted Drakelow Tunnels in Wolverley and some stories from the east of Shropshire where the county borders with the Wolverhampton area.

Interest in ghosts and hauntings has never been greater. A plethora of television programmes document investigations, some serious and some less so, in allegedly haunted locations right across the country and beyond. As an area, the Black Country has more than its fair share of ghostly stories. Some, like the story of Dorothy Beaumont at Dudley Castle can be traced right back to the English Civil War, whilst others such as one of the apparitions seen at the Beacon Hotel in Sedgley are much more contemporary paranormal phenomena.

So, does the large number of stories associated with this region prove that ghosts exist? It depends very much on your point of view. For many people who have never experienced anything which could be described as paranormal for themselves, often no amount of proof will ever be enough. For those who have experienced for themselves any of the mysterious phenomena documented in this book, no further proof is needed.

Within these pages you will find haunted houses, castles, pubs, hotels and a host of other locations carefully researched and mapped by the author over many years. Where known, buildings which no longer exist at the time of publication are noted in the text. Similarly, photographs taken at the time the stories were collected may not necessarily reflect buildings and locations as they appear now. This is particularly true of public houses.

Do take care if you are planning to visit any of these haunted locations in person and please be respectful of both people and places. Very few are private homes but those that are would probably not welcome unwanted intrusion. The vast majority can be visited if you have the nerve but bear in mind some may charge an admission fee if the hauntings are based on a castle or museum site for example. Haunted hostelries of course may be visited during opening hours for nothing more than just the price of a drink.

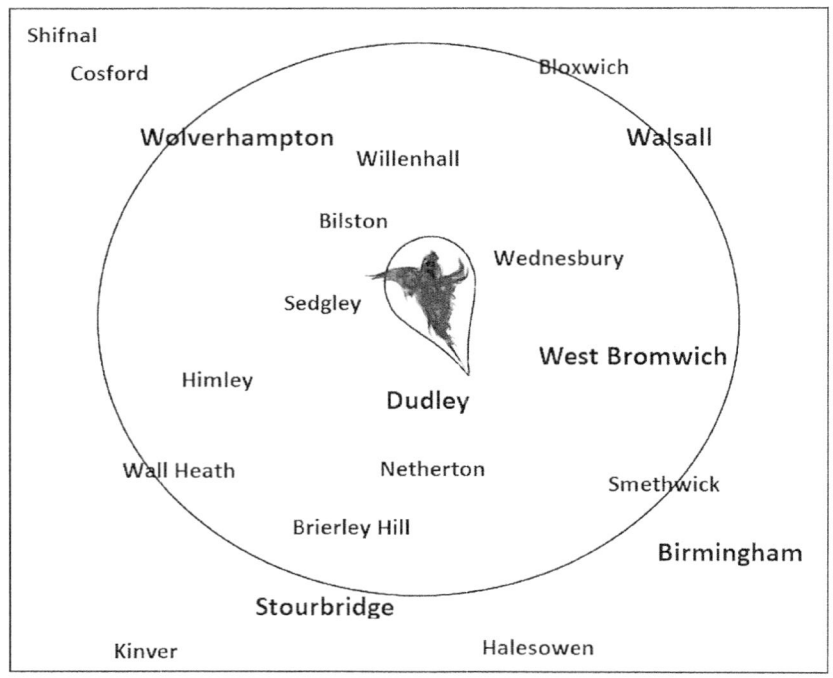

The Black Country and surrounding area

GAZETEER GUIDE TO
BLACK COUNTRY GHOSTS AND HAUNTINGS

The Gazetteer Guide is arranged in alphabetical order by area followed by the individual entries. Each of the entries can be located by address and postcode but longitude and latitude co-ordinates are also given. Used in conjunction with mapping software such as Google Maps and other mapping applications the exact location can be pinpointed. Google Street View and past Street View is available for the majority of entries and enables you to explore using detailed colour pictures simply by dragging the yellow Pegman to the areas surrounding the red pins. Who knows what may be lying hidden away in some of these Street View and past Street View photographs of haunted locations, just waiting to be discovered.

Bilston

Beldray Ltd
Mount Pleasant
Bilston
WV14 7PR

 52.568989, -2.070893

Beldray Ltd dates back to 1872 and specialised in producing brass and copper wares from its Mount Pleasant works and offices. It was originally called Bradley and Company Ltd when it was founded by Walter Smith Bradley. The company later became known as Beldray which is an anagram of Bradley. The company closed in 2005 but the splendid 1930's fronted office building has been preserved.

The apparition reputed to haunt the old office building is known locally as 'The Beldray Ghost'. He is said to be one Hermon Bradley who became Chairman just after the First World War. Hermon passed away in 1955. Since then his presence was felt and sometimes his apparition seen at different times all over the factory but seemed to be particularly active in the offices and especially around the area of the ladies' toilet. Female staff even took to leaving the toilet door unlocked, just in case the ghost of Hermon should put in an appearance.

Hermon had a lifelong liking for fast cars and in his younger days had raced at Brooklands. Perhaps this is why, in 1977, the night security guard doing his rounds near the firm's old garages suddenly found himself face to face with a figure he instantly recognized as being the long dead Hermon Bradley. The guard promptly resigned the following day.

The Olde White Rose
Lichfield Street
Bilston
WV14 0AG

 52.566034, -2.073694

The Olde White Rose was originally a coaching inn dating back to at least the 1700s. Behind the original stable area at the rear was an old printing works which has now been turned into a hotel. On taking over the pub in 1997, landlord John Denston was told by some of the regulars that the pub was haunted, but he would have none of it.

After taking over John had opened up a lengthy disused cellar which had long since been blocked off. There was no clue as to why this particular cellar had been blocked off especially as the far end had a beer drop which was also convenient for lifting the empty barrels up to ground level. After having lights installed it was usable again. It was in this cellar system that John clearly witnessed an apparition early one Thursday morning in the winter of 1998.

John had gone down into the old cellar early to prepare for a beer delivery at around 7.00am. He had turned on the lights and was about to move the empty barrels to the bottom of the drop at the other end. As he stepped into the cellar John clearly saw the figure of a man slide down the beer drop and stand at the end of the old cellar. He was wearing old fashioned and quite well-worn clothes. He had black baggy trousers with a grey buttoned up tunic top. His hair was dark and unruly, his face pale and gaunt and he had particularly bushy eyebrows. After standing stock still for a few moments staring at his upturned palms the man disappeared into a side tunnel. By this time, John realised it must have been an apparition. The man had vanished. The side tunnel went nowhere. It was securely bricked up at the other end.

The Greyhound and Punchbowl
High Street
Bilston
WV14 0EP

 52.563945, -2.080735

The Greyhound and Punchbowl is an ancient pub which has the unusual feature of a tree trunk at its centre. Originally the Manor House of Stow Heath, it is associated with the Mollesley family. Indeed, one member of the family left his mark by carving 'John Mollesley 1483' into a beam in one of the bedrooms.

A number of figures have been sighted here including the 'Punchbowl Ghost' reputed to walk out of the old smoke room clutching a glass of whiskey. A tall man in a black cloak and large black hat has been seen around the kitchen area. He is often mistaken for an intruder but when staff go to investigate further there is never anyone there.

One member of staff had the unnerving experience of entering the pub to find it full of customers. Unnerving because the pub was closed at the time and they all simply vanished away in front of him. A similar experience occurred one night after closing time when two men were seen talking in the corridor before suddenly disappearing in front of the witnesses.

More disturbing is the sound of a baby crying which is clearly heard in the pub sometimes. Local legend has it that the baby is crying for her mother, murdered by a cruel landlord many years ago. The mother is said to wander the pub also, seeking revenge on her murderer.

The Trumpet
High Street
Bilston
WV14 0EP

 52.563837, -2.080445

The Trumpet came into being in 1833 following Wellington's 1830 Beer Act but the building was previously a butchers and slaughterhouse. This Act allowed anyone with 2 Guineas to take out a Beerhouse licence in order to brew and sell their own beer. In the Black Country, many butchers took advantage of this, and so it was with the Trumpet, originally called The Butchers Arms. For many years the pub was called The Royal Exchange. It had the nickname 'Trumpet' when the pub started to become known as a local jazz venue. The nickname stuck, and the pub officially became 'The Trumpet' in 2006.

These days, The Trumpet carries on a great jazz atmosphere which attracts enthusiasts from far and wide, but sometimes takes on a much more supernatural one. Cold spots, mysterious bangs and flashing lights have all been experienced here. The staff have also reported feeling uneasy when working on their own in the cellar at times as if someone was down there with them, close by and watching but so far unseen. A previous barmaid became so terrified after her experience of the malevolent atmosphere in the cellar that she immediately put her coat on and left. No amount of persuasion could convince her to ever work in the pub ever again.

The White Rose
Temple Street
Bilston
WV14 0NU

 52.563451, -2.069523

The White Rose is now sadly demolished and a new housing development has been built on the site. Lizzie, a previous landlady, reputedly haunted the former White Rose. She liked to make herself known when new staff took over, but it was not always a pleasant welcome. One previous landlord packed his bags and immediately left after the ghost of Lizzie appeared to him in the cellar and threw something at him. She had also been known to call out the names of staff from somewhere down below in the cellar.

Low level poltergeist activity was also a feature of the pub with things disappearing and then suddenly appearing again in an obvious place. On one occasion, a purse went missing only to reappear in a bedroom which had already been thoroughly searched.

Some nights, the pub had been heard to come alive again as if the bar were full in the early hours of the morning. When staff went down to investigate the noise would suddenly stop. A shadowy figure was also a regular visitor. He would be seen walking past the bar door into the lounge. Needless to say, when anyone went to look the lounge was empty with nowhere the shadowy figure could have gone.

The paranormal activity here appears to have been wholly associated with the earlier pub building and there have been no further reports from the area.

Bloxwich

Maternity Hospital
Reeves Street
Bloxwich
WS3 2JJ

 52.613255, -2.004398

Bloxwich Maternity Hospital is now used to care for elderly people. The building dates back to 1850 where it started life as a private house known as the Manor House. Walsall Corporation purchased the property in 1927 from the Foster family who had owned it during the late Victorian and Edwardian period. The house was subsequently turned into a maternity hospital in 1929. Then known as the Maternity and Child Welfare Hospital it became Bloxwich Maternity Home from 1948 until 1981.

During its time as a maternity hospital there were reports that the building was haunted. In addition to the midwives employed there a lady was regularly seen or her presence felt. This happened so often that she was given the nickname 'Florrie'. Florrie seems to have been particularly attached to the staff, and in particular the area in and around the midwives' staff room.

She does not seem to have been at all frightening as those who saw or experienced her presence invariably described Florrie as being completely benign. By all accounts these visitations carried on for many years. It is not known whether 'Florrie' was associated with the earlier days of the Maternity Hospital or perhaps the Foster family such as one of the 'Misses Foster' who lived in the house up until around 1916 and possibly never left.

Spring Cottage
Elmore Green Road
Bloxwich
WS3 2HN

 52.617055, -2.009028

The Spring Cottage of today dates back to the late 1850s but has been subject to alteration since then including a major rebuild in 1901. The cottage immediately next door was incorporated in the late 1940s to further extend the pub.

The Spring Cottage was reputedly used as a temporary gaol for prisoners in Victorian times. They would be incarcerated in the cellar where there was no chance of escape. This is a claim made by many pubs right across the Black Country but as the original Bloxwich Police Station was also built on Elmore Green Road in 1884 there is a at least a local connection to early policing.

Whether the ghost who haunts The Spring Cottage is associated with these earlier miscreants, a former resident or even an old pub customer is subject to conjecture. However, the building is prone to strange noises particularly at night, and more rarely a fleeting figure is seen. Heavy footsteps coming from upstairs are sometimes heard by both staff and customers alike, even when the rooms are known to be empty. The cause of these heavy footsteps can never be traced. As soon as anyone is brave enough to go upstairs to investigate it all falls quiet again, just as it should be.

Wallington Heath
Bloxwich
WS3 3RF

 52.624833, -2.003167

Wallington Heath was once the site of a coaching inn called The Old Kings Arms. In later years, it became a convent of St. Paul of Chartres until the building was closed in the 1960s to make way for a housing development. One of the ghost stories here relates back to the time of the old inn when coaches would regularly stop to water their horses in the pool here.

One particularly stormy night the coachman decided it would be unwise to carry on further and arranged for his passengers to spend the night at the Old Kings Arms. A young French lady was travelling on her own and carrying a roll of silk which was a valuable commodity in those days. After a meal at the inn everyone retired for the night expecting to make an early start the following morning. When morning came, there was no sign of the young lady or one of the horsemen. She had been brutally robbed and murdered during the night, her body mutilated almost beyond recognition.

Local legend has it that her spirit has never left. On certain nights, she can be seen by the pool quietly weeping under one of the trees. Few people who knew the story would dare to linger there for long after dark.

The area is also renowned for a ghost known as 'The Flying Nun of Bloxwich'. She is said to have been a nun at the former convent who committed suicide by drowning herself in one of the nearby pools. The misty figure of her ghost is said to float silently above the water where she took her own life.

Brierley Hill

Queens Head
Level Street
Brierley Hill
DY5 1UA

 52.484991, -2.111514

The Queen's Head in Brierley Hill is no longer a public house but was once owned by the Earl of Dudley. When it was a pub there were several local stories associated with it. It was reputed to be haunted by one Jonathon Maughan, but little is known about him or why he should have been haunting The Queen's Head except that he was said to have a particularly mean streak. Another story has it that there is a secret escape tunnel under the pub although it must be said stories of secret tunnels under public houses are commonplace.

Back in the days when it was a pub a relief manager and his wife were rudely awoken one night by the sound of heavy furniture being moved around in the bar. They warily went downstairs to see what was happening and found nothing. No sign of anything being moved and all the doors and windows still securely locked and bolted. They would probably not have known about the story of the secret tunnel or the fact that the licensee they were standing in for had a dog who would never go anywhere near the entrance to the cellar, growling as if someone or something was lying in wait down below.

Colley Gate

Little Chop House
Windmill Hill
Colley Gate
B63 2BZ

 52.458775, -2.083985

The Little Chop House used to be known as The White Lion. George Stafford was landlord of the pub for many years from the 1920s onwards. George had another occupation, that of local undertaker. In fact, he was known to make his coffins at the rear of the pub. The ghost here though appears to come from an earlier time.

When the pub was taken over by new licensees in 1999 they received a welcome they were certainly not expecting. At times doors would open and close on their own, mysterious footsteps would be heard in the bar and objects, such as the landlord's watch, would disappear and then reappear in unexpected places. Even more disturbing, one of the beds would dip as if someone were sitting on it. The couple soon got to hear about the little girl who allegedly haunted the pub and the fact that new licensees were sure to experience her presence.

The story was that the little girl had died of Scarlet Fever in 1903 and the distraught parents had sealed off the bedroom in which she passed away. The paranormal activity continued unabated until the pub underwent a major refurbishment. During these alterations, a startling discovery was made. Builders knocked through a wall and discovered a small sealed off room, just big enough to have been a child's bedroom. Strangely enough, after the hidden room was discovered everything quietened down. For now at least.

Coseley

Coseley Canal Tunnel
Ivyhouse Lane
Coseley
WV14 9JH

 52.543719, -2.088099

The ghost that reputedly haunts Coseley Canal Tunnel is known as the White Lady. Her apparition is seen staring silently into the water. The local story is that the White Lady is one Hannah Johnson Cox who lived with her husband and five children around 1900. Hannah was suffering from depression after the birth of her last child. Losing their home through her feckless husband's drinking and gambling was the last straw.

In 1901, whilst in a deeply depressed state she drowned her two youngest daughters, Flora Jane and Mary Madeline Cox in the canal. She tied them up in an apron and pushed them under the water near to the entrance of the Coseley Tunnel. Having done this the distraught Hannah promptly gave herself up to the local Police. A desperate attempt was made to rescue the two little girls but although they had already been pulled out of the water by local boatmen it was too late. They were already dead.

Taking into account her mental state and the strength of public sympathy Hannah escaped the gallows but ended up in a mental asylum. Her husband, Philip Cox, was largely blamed by local people and forced to flee for his life. He ended up in America and was twice more married despite never divorcing his first wife. Hannah was released from the asylum in 1906 and lived out her life with her brothers and remaining children before passing away in 1948.

Old Meeting Road
Coseley
WV14 8HB

 52.542980, -2.084014

During the industrial revolution, Coseley was one of a number of coal mining areas in the Black Country. There were many small pits in operation in and around Coseley many of them roughly following the line of the Birmingham Canal. The coal mines are now long gone with the last pit in the old Black Country, Baggeridge Colliery, closing in 1968. Baggeridge was situated in the quaintly named Gospel End Village which, like Coseley, was part of the ancient Manor of Sedgley.

Paranormal activity used to be reported in the former Youth Centre on Old Meeting Road which was destroyed by fire in 2009. Items disappearing and reappearing were common, and the sounds of movement coming from inside the locked building used to be heard when there was nobody there.

Old Meeting Road itself seems to have retained an echo of its industrial past in the form of an apparition seen walking along here. He is a coal miner, dressed for work. A hard-working man still following his old familiar route in the direction of the Birmingham Canal as he did in life. Mining was a hazardous occupation at the best of times and many men lost their lives underground. Perhaps this is the reason why he is never seen returning home from his shift at the pit.

Cradley Heath

Haden Hill House
Halesowen Road
Cradley Heath
B64 7JU

 52.468024, -2.062460

Haden Hill House is now a museum open to the public in Haden Hill Park. The museum is housed in the Victorian residence built in 1878. The Victorian building is attached to Haden Old Hall which dates back to the 1600s.

Haden Hill has a number of ghost stories associated with it and shares one with Hales Abbey at Halesowen (see page 57). There is said to be a tunnel leading from Haden Hill to Hales Abbey once used by a young lady Elaine and her lover, a monk from the Abbey. It is a distance of some two and a half miles which makes such a tunnel extremely unlikely to ever have existed.

Even so, Haden Hill is famously haunted by a lady dressed in white who has been seen both in the house and around the grounds. She is also seen peering out of the upstairs windows of the old hall when there is nobody supposed to be in the building.

A likely candidate for the white lady ghost is Ann Eliza Haden. She was the last member of the Haden family to live in the old hall. She was a spinster who devoted her life to protecting her beloved Haden Hall from the onslaught of the industrial revolution all around it. She passed away in the hall in 1876. Given her love for the estate it would be rather fitting if Eliza was still keeping a watch on her former home.

Darlaston

Saint Lawrence's Churchyard
Church Street
Darlaston
WS10 8ES  52.569133, -2.035411

It is not the church but the churchyard which has a rather unusual story attached to it. In the churchyard, there is a large statue of a mother and child by sculptor Thomas Wright. The statue was commissioned by Darlaston Urban District Council and unveiled in 1958. It was erected to commemorate Harry Bishop Marston who was a local businessman and long serving council member.

There have been numerous reports, and some of them from multiple witnesses, that the child ceases to be made of stone and walks around the churchyard separate from the mother who remains a figure in stone. As if that wasn't enough the statue has also been seen to glow in the dark.

Other sightings too are linked with the churchyard. The main one being that of a monk dressed in a white habit. He has also been seen wandering the grounds. The present-day building stands on the site of a much earlier church dating back to at least the 12th century. The white monk may be associated with this earlier time or he may even be a Chantry Priest, known to have been present in Darlaston, and paid to sing masses for the salvation of souls in the days before the dissolution of the monasteries by Henry VIII.

Dudley

Baylies Hall
Tower Street
Dudley
DY1 1NB

 52.512250, -2.081836

Baylies Hall Charity School was founded in 1732 by Robert, Samuel and Anne Baylies for 'teaching, instructing, and clothing 50 boys, to be elected and chosen out of the parishes of town and foreign of Dudley from such whose parents would not be able to give them learning'. In recent years, it again had an educational function when nearby Dudley College (see page 33) used it as extra teaching space. The building is Grade II listed and is currently being used as an auction house.

During the time that Dudley College had the building some students chose to play with a Ouija board during their lunch break. They thought they had got in touch with a little girl who said she was lost and alone in the building. Some of the students were very upset by this and needed counselling after playing with the board.

However, this was not an end to it as from then on lone staff locking up the building at night would sometimes hear what sounded like a child crying coming from somewhere down in the cellars. Despite hearing this on a number of occasions nobody ever had the nerve to go down into the cellars on their own to see who or what it was.

Black Country Living Museum
Tipton Road
Dudley
DY1 4SQ

 52.519700, -2.074911

With such a large number of old buildings it is no surprise that the Black Country Living Museum has had reports of unusual happenings. There have been at least three reports in broad daylight of a wounded soldier seen sitting in the first classroom of St James's School. As soon as he is noticed the figure disappears. There is a military connection with the school as American soldiers were billeted there prior to the D-Day landings.

Early one morning a member of staff was walking past the Chemist shop. She noticed three old ladies in authentic Victorian dresses chatting inside. Assuming they were costumed staff she looked away but on looking back the ladies had vanished. A path runs between the Chemist shop and the Chapel. It is here that a tall, slim lady in a period black dress has been seen again by museum staff. As soon as they look away and glance back the lady is gone.

The Toll House, dating back to 1845, is another building where strange things are reported. Very often visitors will ask if one particular room is haunted. It is always the bedroom on the right. On one occasion, a lady asked if she could look in the bedroom as the door was closed. She opened the door and quickly closed it. When asked why she hadn't gone in the lady said she didn't want to disturb the girl sleeping on the bed. The room was empty.

Bottle and Glass Inn
Tipton Road
Dudley
DY1 4SQ

 52.523302, -2.077225

The Bottle and Glass public house was moved from its original location in Brockmoor to the Black Country Living Museum where it backed onto the canal as it does now. When the pub has been shut up a man described as having a very round face and wearing circular glasses has been seen peering out of one of the windows.

The sound of someone moving around in the back room is regularly heard by pub staff even though they know the room is empty. Staff also sometimes have the experience of someone tapping on their shoulder. Of course, when they turn around there is no-one there.

Female staff in costume sometimes have their long dresses firmly pulled as if by a child. This may be the same child who has been seen in and around the pub. The child is said to be ten-year-old Isaac Male. Back when the canals were busy with horse drawn working barges Isaac worked for boatman James Haines. One very foggy night Haines and two of his men were leading their horse back to its stable. In the dense fog, the horse lost its footing and fell into the canal with young Isaac clinging desperately to its back. The only thing Haines and his men cared about was rescuing their valuable horse. It was something like twenty minutes before they got the horse out of the canal and finally turned their attention to Isaac. It was too late, he had already drowned. The inquest was held in the Bottle and Glass and a verdict of accidental death was delivered. However, Haines and his men were severely criticised for allowing poor Isaac to drown that night. Reason enough for young Isaac to still make his presence felt in the Bottle and Glass.

Blue Coat School
Beechwood Road
Dudley
DY2 7QA

 52.511711, -2.069790

In 1970 The Blue Coat School which was established in 1869 took over the buildings of Rosland Secondary School. The Rosland School buildings themselves were built in 1932. When the Bluecote School closed in 1989 some of the old buildings formed part of a community network centre which itself closed in 2015.

One part of the old Blue Coat School had quite a reputation for being haunted. The teacher's staff room was situated on a landing up a flight of stairs. It was on this landing that a tall, dark looking figure was sighted on a number of occasions. He would be standing still and looking down over the bannister as if checking on the behaviour of pupils passing by beneath. The assumption is that he was the ghost of one of the old teachers or even the headmaster although there is no evidence to support this.

One morning, the caretaker was on his own unlocking the building ready for the day ahead. After opening up the area where the old staffroom used to be he glanced up to see that the tall man was on the landing looking down at him. Initially thinking it was an intruder, the caretaker shouted at the man who simply faded away.

Dudley Canal Tunnel

Birmingham New Road
Dudley
DY1 4SB

 52.523192, -2.079020

Dudley Canal Tunnel opened in October, 1792. The narrow tunnel had no towpath and boats would be 'legged' through by men lying on their backs and walking along the walls. These days the Dudley Canal and Tunnel Trust run boat trips through the tunnels and caverns.

After the first section from the entrance the boat passes through the Shirts Mill Basin and the Castle Mill Basin. It is around here that the ghosts of two children have been heard near to the entrance of the Wren's Nest Tunnel. The youngsters had tried to get through the tunnel on a home-made raft and perished in the attempt. The unmistakable sounds of children laughing are heard together with a boat being paddled. Just as it seems that they are emerging from the disused tunnel, the noises fade away and all is quiet again.

Another child haunting the caverns is twelve-year-old Freddie Lester from Netherton. He was bird nesting in the 1950s when he slipped and fell into the caverns well beyond any hope of rescue.

Bob Dale was down in the caverns on his own changing some lights. He had climbed up the ladder and was in full view of the manageress through the CCTV system. The internal phone went, and the manageress asked who else was down there. Bob said no-one, but the manageress had clearly seen someone holding the bottom of the ladder for Bob.

The Manageress was once down in the tunnels on her own and radioed for someone to come quickly and collect her. She had clearly seen a figure walking above the water. He may have been one of the men tragically killed in a roof fall on the last day of mining in Hurst Cavern. Echoes of these long deceased miners are sometimes heard working and singing in the caverns.

Dudley Zoo and Castle
Castle Hill
Dudley
DY1 4QF    52.513269, -2.077558

S everal of ghosts are said to haunt Dudley Zoo and Castle. The Round House near to the main entrance to the zoo has been subject to much paranormal activity. A few years back Chris Jeans, 'Bonkers the clown', was lodged in the Round House during the summer season. He was disturbed one night by the ghost of a legless, middle aged man in his bedroom who asked, "why have you returned?". After that Chris took to sleeping in his car.

There have been lots of reports of a lone figure who walks the battlements of Dudley Castle at night. Whoever the ghost is there have been some plausible witnesses. On one occasion, the police were called as it was thought an intruder had got into the grounds. One officer stayed beneath the keep in case anyone tried to run away and another officer climbed up to see if anyone was on the battlements. When he  came back down the first officer demanded to know where the miscreant was. It turns out that from down below he had seen two figures walking along the top of the keep whereas the officer who climbed up had seen nothing.

The Queen Mary Ballroom has its own phantom pianist. Only heard when the building is locked up and otherwise quiet the unmistakeable sound of a piano playing has been clearly heard.

The castle Undercroft, beneath the Chapel, is home to two stone coffins. As was witnessed by a cleaner early one morning, a pair of knee length boots are seen standing in the larger coffin. According to the astonished cleaner the boots gradually faded away as she watched in disbelief.

Dudley Castle Grey Lady
Castle Hill
Dudley
DY1 4QF

 52.514026, -2.079933

Perhaps the most well-known ghost haunting Dudley Castle is that of Dorothy Beaumont. She is better known as the 'Grey Lady' who haunts the area around the base of the castle keep forlornly searching for her husband and child. She was the wife of the Deputy Commander of Royalist forces at the castle during the siege by Parliamentarian soldiers in 1646. Dorothy gave birth to a daughter, Frances, in 1645 but the child only survived a few months and her body was buried at St Edmunds, known locally as 'bottom church'.

Dorothy never recovered from this loss and passed away herself during the siege. Her body could not be buried with that of her daughter as Colonel Leveson, commander of the Royalist forces, had the church destroyed prior to the siege to stop it being used as a vantage point by the Parliamentarians. Dorothy's body was permitted to be taken through the Parliamentarian lines to be buried at St Thomas's Church, known locally as 'top church'. Her husband was not allowed to accompany the funeral procession.

The sad and lonely ghost of Dorothy Beaumont now roams the castle grounds and the keep. Dudley Zoo and Castle used to host regular ghost walks here using actors and actresses to play the parts of the ghosts. More than once visitors reported seeing a second 'Grey Lady' on the castle keep in addition to the actress playing her. It seems Dorothy Beaumont herself would sometimes put in a spectral appearance during these evening ghost walks.

Dudley College
The Broadway
Dudley
DY1 4AS

 52.514087, -2.083656

Given its location in allegedly the most haunted area of Dudley just below Dudley Castle it comes as no surprise that the Broadway Site of Dudley College has stories of hauntings. Footsteps resound along the empty corridors on C Floor and doors are prone to opening and closing on their own. The goods lift too at the rear of the building goes up and down on its own at times even though no electrical fault can be found.

In keeping with its close proximity to the ruined Dudley Priory, a black monk has been seen on numerous occasions in different parts of the building. The sound of keys jangling as if someone were walking past reception is heard as a long dead caretaker still does his evening rounds.

The ghost of a slight, rather dapper gentleman in a dark suit carrying a rectangular briefcase has been seen walking briskly into one of the rooms on B-Floor. One witness, James, saw the figure early one morning. "He was a few yards ahead of me and walked straight into room B-15. On checking the room there was nobody there and nowhere the gentleman could have gone."

The room in question was used to teach mine engineering up until the early 1960s and the long dead mining lecturer, Sam Thompson, matches the description of the phantom figure with the briefcase. Apparently, he always used to arrive early for work to prepare the day's lessons.

Dudley Hippodrome
Castle Hill
Dudley
DY1 4RA

 52.513536, -2.076151

Dudley Hippodrome opened in 1938 and replaced the earlier Dudley Opera House which was destroyed by fire in 1937. It was a popular venue for many stars such as Bob Hope, Laurel and Hardy, George Formby and a veritable host of others. Frequently they would stay at The Station Hotel opposite (see page 45). Variety shows continued up until 1964 and then the building became a bingo hall. Currently a local support group is fighting to stop the now disused Art Deco building from being demolished.

During its time as a bingo hall particularly there were reports that the building was haunted. Staff would see figures moving about in the auditorium when there should have been no one there. Taps would turn on in the toilets for no reason and cold spots felt in various rooms around the venue. On occasions in certain rooms staff would get the distinct feeling that they were not alone.

One story from the building's earlier life as a theatre may have a bearing on the paranormal activity experienced here. It concerns a young lady who fell deeply in love with a handsome actor. After a passionate affair he left her without even bothering to say goodbye. Heartbroken, the young lady is said to have committed suicide by hanging herself upstairs in the building.

Dudley Priory
The Broadway
Dudley
DY1 4AY

 52.515397, -2.084806

Dudley Priory was founded around 1150 by Gervase Paganel and was closed by Henry VIII during the dissolution of the monasteries in the 16th century. The Dudley Priory of Cluniac monks was dedicated to St James. Nowadays all that remains is a ruin located in Priory Park which is Grade II listed by English Heritage.

As with Benedictine monks, Cluniac monks were also known as 'black monks' due to the black robe worn over their habits. The ghosts of black monks have been seen at various locations on Castle Hill including the nearby Dudley College (see page 33) and Dudley Castle (see page 31). Not surprisingly, they are also seen and heard within the ruined Priory itself. Whilst ghostly monks are a commonly reported apparition, nevertheless it is only ever black monks which are seen around Castle Hill. Never white monks, the similarly attired but white robed monks of the Cistercian Order.

Sometimes they are clearly seen or more usually observed only as fleeting figures often just seen out of the corner of the eye and quickly disappearing behind the ruins. Listen carefully in the vicinity of the old Priory and you may be lucky enough to hear the faint, eerie sounds of monks chanting. A distant echo of the past somehow manifesting in the present day.

Green Man Entry
Castle Street
Dudley
DY1 1LQ

 52.512152, -2.080479

The Green Man Entry is a passageway leading from Castle Street to Tower Street and dating back to medieval times. The name comes from the former Green Man public house dating back to 1793 which was situated above and to the right of the passageway. The entry was once adorned with a magnificent Green Man foliate head cast in bronze, believed to be a symbol of the spring and rebirth. Sadly, the sculpture disappeared sometime in 2012.

The former Green Man public house was reputed to be haunted, and so it is with the entry. From Castle Street, the other end of the passageway leads down towards the side of The Malt Shovel on Tower Street.

The entry is haunted by the ghost of a man wearing old fashioned working clothes and a cap who is always seen to enter from the Tower Street side. He then suddenly disappears before reaching the Castle Street end. This same figure has been seen a number of times including by a student of the nearby Dudley College. She was making her way home after an evening class and was just behind the man as he went into the entry. She noted his old fashioned attire but did not realise it was an apparition she was seeing until entering the passageway herself. The oddly dressed man in front of her had suddenly vanished. He could never have reached Castle Street in such a short space of time and there was nowhere else he could possibly have gone.

JB's Nightclub
King Street
Dudley
DY2 8PX

52.507994, -2.086998

JB's Nightclub in Dudley used to be situated immediately behind the old Pathfinder building in King Street. The club was renowned for giving up and coming bands an opportunity to play from the early 1970s before moving to Castle Hill, Dudley in 1994. The whole area around the old club in King Street had a reputation for being haunted (see also Vicar Street, page 46).

The ghost here was reputed to be a young man dressed in First World War military uniform who was regularly seen by staff and club goers. It is not at all clear who the young man might be or why he should be haunting JB's. However, one version of the story has it that the young man voluntarily resigned his teaching position at a local school to march off proudly to war, only to die in the trenches not long after.

The school story may have some credibility. Teachers were exempt from being conscripted in the First World War. Also, it is not immediately obvious that the old Pathfinder Menswear building, which is now a Hindu Temple, used to be St Thomas's National School established in 1847. Or that JB's Nightclub had taken over one of the old school buildings.

The Malt Shovel
Tower Street
Dudley
DY1 1NB

52.512448, -2.081897

The Malt Shovel dates back to at least 1819 and used to be known as The Lord Wellington, Old Malt Shovel and finally The Malt Shovel. It was also known locally as the 'Madhouse'. The pub is situated in one of the most haunted areas of Dudley. Both Baylies Hall and the Green Man Entry adjacent to the pub are subject to paranormal activity.

In 1926 the pub was the scene of a brutal murder. Fourteen-year-old Jimmy Bayliss, son of Mr and Mrs Trevor Bayliss of the Malt Shovel, was found battered to death in his bed. The left side of his face had been smashed with an axe. His half-brother, Joseph Edward Flavell (Eddie), confessed to the murder but escaped the gallows when his defence successfully entered a plea of madness.

Since then, a ghost known as the Blue Boy, is seen in the upstairs windows of the pub. This apparition is usually seen as an indistinct, misty form. Another apparition seen here is a slightly built adult who walks through the pub sometimes accompanied by a black dog. When staff go to look where they have gone they are nowhere to be seen.

Customers have been known to be pushed in the back by unseen hands and at times glasses shake violently or fly off their hooks for no apparent reason. When the author was interviewing the landlady here some time back all of the glasses hanging above the bar started to swing for no apparent reason, just as if someone was wanting to make their presence known.

Priory Hall
Priory Road
Dudley
DY1 4EU

52.516757, -2.086589

P riory Hall dates back to 1825 when it was built by the Earl of Dudley of the time. The Tudor Gothic style residence was originally intended to serve as a town house for the Earl and his family or as a dower house, but subsequently it housed one of his senior estate managers. The hall was acquired by Dudley Borough Council in 1926 and these days the Grade II listed Priory Hall is used as Dudley Register Office. The hall stands in the grounds of the ruined Dudley Priory which itself is haunted (see page 35). It is frequently used as the setting for wedding photographs.

Priory Hall is said to be haunted by the ghost of a small child. As far as is known this apparition is only ever seen from the outside of the building. Usually when the building is closed, the face of what appears to be a child has been seen peering intently out from one of the windows overlooking the Priory ruins. Who the child is or what period he or she might come from is not known.

Snapshots taken in Priory Park looking towards Priory Hall sometimes contain an unexpected extra, the face of the mysterious phantom child.

Shrewsbury Arms
Wolverhampton Street
Dudley
DY1 1DA

52.509898, -2.084059

The Shrewsbury Arms is a town centre pub which can trace its history back to 1819, when it was known as The Talbot Hotel. Locally it is known by its nickname, 'The Cow Shed'. There are various theories as to why it got this name which has stuck over the years.

There is a possibility that the old building was once part of a farm. Another theory has it that there used to be a slaughterhouse right next door. During Victorian times the pub had something of a reputation for being a house of ill repute. Any or none of these might explain the rather unusual nickname.

The pub is haunted by a seemingly benign chap nicknamed Old Joe. He is a figure in a cloth cap who has been seen in the cellar and walking around the bar after the pub is closed. He has been seen by a number of people over the years but there is no clue as to why he is associated with the pub. In the 1980s one of the bar staff, Marlene, clearly saw the apparition of an old man in a cloth cap standing looking at her.

He was given the name Old Joe by staff at the pub who are convinced that he is something to do with a long-lost slaughterhouse next door rather than being a previous landlord or customer. Of course, if the building was once a farm Old Joe could be associated with that.

Sir Gilbert Claughton School
Blowers Green Road
Dudley
DY2 8UZ

52.504446, -2.091640

A rather strange report comes from Blowers Green Road very near to the former Sir Gilbert Claughton School which closed in 1990. It is not the old school building itself that is haunted as far as is known, but the wasteland which once bordered it.

The report concerns a young man from Dudley who was courting his girlfriend and future wife who lived in Netherton. One particular night William, known as Billy, missed the last bus home and decided to walk back. He walked up through Cinder Bank and on to Blowers Green Road. It was getting on for midnight by the time he was walking up towards the school.

On his right-hand side, an old set of railings separated the path from some waste land beyond. He became aware of a figure striding quickly across the open land diagonally towards him. The figure got closer and closer to the railings but instead of stopping simply passed straight through. As if that wasn't frightening enough the figure halted for a moment and stared straight at Billy. He had the face of a pig! By this time the young man had seen enough and ran all the way back home without stopping or looking back.

St Edmund's Churchyard
Castle Street
Dudley
DY1 4PS

52.511833, -2.080500

Saint Edmund's Church is better known locally as 'bottom church'. It was rebuilt in 1724 after being demolished in 1646 by Colonel Leveson to avoid it being used by Parliamentarian troops during the final siege of Dudley Castle in the English Civil War.

The church is associated with a local hangman, Edward Croaker, who is buried in the churchyard there. Local legend maintains that at the stroke of midnight the ghost of Edward Croaker rises up from his grave to be pursued by the shades of those he had executed.

One popular story of 'Croaker's Ghost' concerned a group of young men drinking in the nearby Hawke's Head Inn. They dared one of their number to spend the hour after midnight sitting on Croaker's grave for a bet. In order to prove he had done it the young man was to leave his dagger plunged in the earth over the grave.

The drunken young man was seen to enter the churchyard but no one else had the nerve to stay around to witness the deed. The next morning the young man was missing. A search revealed his corpse laid out alongside Croaker's grave with a look of sheer terror on his face. The young man had died of shock, his dagger plunged through his own cloak into the earth. Naturally this story added greatly to the ghostly legend of Edward Croaker.

The Court House
New Street
Dudley
DY1 1LP

52.511570, -2.082738

The Court House used to be known as The Court House Tavern and dates back to at least 1854. If you enjoy cider as well as real ales this is definitely the place to visit as it regularly gets voted Cider Pub of the Year. Given that it is situated in one of the most haunted parts of Dudley, not surprisingly a range of paranormal phenomena has been experienced here over the years.

Much of the activity here is auditory although figures have also been seen in the pub. Loud inexplicable noises come from the cellar when there is no one down there. Staff are very familiar with the normal everyday sounds which come from the pub cellar and are equally well aware when something doesn't sound quite right, although they can never determine exactly what the noises are. They never seem to occur when staff are working down there.

Names are often heard being called from the room upstairs again when there is nobody up there. Often the names being called are not known but sometimes they are existing staff members. Some years ago, Gail, who was working at the pub would regularly hear her name called.

Staff and customers have also witnessed beer glasses being lifted off the shelf and held in the air before being smashed to the floor. A figure of a man has also been seen coming into the pub and walking straight through the bar. However, when the staff go to check they invariably find that there is nobody there and nowhere the figure could have gone except back through the bar where he would have been seen.

The Old Priory
New Street
Dudley
DY1 1LU

52.511649, -2.083297

The Old Priory is recorded as being a hostelry as early as 1820. At that time, it was known as The Nag's Head. As with the majority of Black Country public houses at that time the brewing of beer took place on the premises in the brewhouse or 'brew'uss' in the local dialect.

In common with many other pubs glasses are prone to being thrown off the shelves and loud sounds are heard coming from the cellar when there is no-one down there. In this case the noises are easily identifiable. It is the unmistakable sound of barrels being moved around in the empty cellar. When staff go down to check of course the noises stop and there is no sign of anything untoward having taken place.

A few years back, two relief managers were unfortunate enough to encounter the phantom lady who resides upstairs in the pub. She is prone to opening the windows, even in winter, and walks up and down the landing at night. Having closed up for the night the two managers retired to their respective rooms upstairs. They were not to get much sleep. They were both terrified by the constant sound of footsteps walking up and down past their bedroom doors. On this particular night, it got so bad that they ended up cowering together in one room. The relief managers couldn't leave the pub fast enough, vowing never to return.

The Station Hotel
Castle Hill
Dudley
DY1 4RA

52.513159, -2.075865

The original Station Hotel was partially open by 1878 providing a service to the local railway station and the Opera House opposite which opened its doors in 1899. The hotel had an extensive network of tunnels beneath which were mainly preserved when the hotel was extensively modernised and enlarged circa 1936. Sadly, many earlier records have been lost making it difficult to confirm or otherwise hotel folklore.

The Station Hotel lays claim to a number of ghosts and a particularly tragic story. A lecherous landlord ordered a young servant girl down into the cellars ostensibly to look for a leg of pork. The landlord tried to have his wicked way with the girl, but she bravely resisted his unwanted advances whilst threatening to tell his wife. In his rage, the landlord clubbed and strangled the unfortunate girl to death and hid her body in a barrel. Her anguished screams are sometimes heard to this day coming from the depths of the cellars. On occasions staff going down into the cellars experience an unseen entity brushing quickly past. The errant landlord perhaps, leaving the scene of his grisly crime.

Hotel rooms in and around 214 are also haunted by a gentleman dressed in black who wears a pointed hat. Guests have woken up in the early hours of the morning to see him standing silently by the bedroom window before disappearing. Expect poltergeist activity in Room 217. You might be rudely awoken by the bed shaking and the lights flashing on and off!

Vicar Street
Dudley
DY2 8RG

52.506800, -2.085150

Vicar Street and the area surrounding it has a long reputation for haunted buildings (see also JB's Nightclub page 37). When the author was working in education in the 1980s he was often required to visit the nearby Dudley Education and Training Centre (DETC). There were many stories of the building being haunted particularly by a well-dressed gentleman who was seen regularly by staff in many parts of the building.

The Locomotive, formerly The Boilermakers Arms which was on Vicar Street is no longer a working pub having closed in the 1970s. However, this building had a reputation for poltergeist activity. Doors would open and close on their own, furniture would be moved and on occasions an entity would be physically felt. A previous landlady had the experience of feeling a strong invisible hand on her shoulder whilst she was changing a barrel in the cellar. A barmaid, who was living there at the time, had the terrifying experience of someone sitting on her bed and trying to pull the bedclothes away from her.

The poltergeist activity was always worse when changes were being made leading to the belief that a former landlord was not happy when 'his' pub was being altered.

Enville

The Cat Inn
Bridgnorth Road
Enville
DY7 5HA

52.478489, -2.257817

The ghost story of The Cat Inn at Enville concerns an old tramp, Billy Pitt, who collapsed in the snow one bitter cold night in mid-winter. Billy was trying to make his way to the Seisdon Union Workhouse at Trysull in the hope of finding a little warmth and sustenance there. The howling of Jim, Billy's dog, brought a group of ne'er-do-wells out of the inn to see what was going on. They dragged Billy into the pub and revived him by the fire.

Thinking to have some sport with the old vagrant they plied him with strong drink until ordered out of the pub by the landlord at closing time. The drunken rabble locked poor old Billy in the stocks and strangled his dog nearby to silence his howling. The following morning the bodies of both Billy and Jim were found frozen to death in the snow.

Since then, the ghosts of both Billy and his dog are said to haunt the village around The Cat Inn searching for their cruel tormenters. At certain times, the chilling howl of a dog is heard to split the night air. This is very much a ghost story in the traditional style (see the Starving Rascal page 104). Nevertheless, a spectral figure has been seen crossing the main Bridgnorth Road in the direction of the pub, seemingly oblivious to the presence of modern day traffic.

Gornal

Bush Inn
Summit Place
Gornal
DY3 2TG

52.515727, -2.135557

The Bush Inn dates back to the Georgian period and was first licenced in 1820 to Stephen Hale. From 1845 to 1854 Mrs Nancy Hale is listed as the licensee. As an inn, it is facing the wrong way round. The original Georgian frontage is now at the rear of the present building.

The pub has a long history of strange phenomena. The sounds of barrels being moved, and loud bangs have been experienced here. An ornamental plate was flung from the wall only to land intact some feet away. The sounds of heavy footsteps coming from the attic have also been heard on occasions.

At least two female apparitions have been seen here together with a dog who likes nothing better than to brush around the legs of staff and customers, unseen of course. A lady in what has been described as Victorian dress has been seen in the pub as has a little old lady. The lady in Victorian dress was seen to glide across the floor in one of the bedrooms on the ground floor. At the time of the sighting she appeared to be floating a little beneath the existing floor level. Hardly surprising as the original floor had been raised during a refurbishment. The Victorian lady is said to be Nancy Hale who of course has every right to be in the pub as she was once the licensee.

Perhaps Nancy and the older lady like to get together for a chat, which might explain the disembodied female voices which have been heard talking in the room which was once reserved just for the ladies.

Ellowes Hall
Ellowes Hall Wood
Gornal
DY3 3XS

52.530393, -2.123500

Ellowes Hall was built in 1821 and was an imposing stately home occupying landscaped parkland near Lower Gornal. The hall was originally the home of wealthy ironmaster Samuel Fereday up until 1850. It was subsequently owned by a succession of wealthy local families.

The stately home was demolished in 1964 to make way for Ellowes Hall School which still exists on the site. Very little remains to show that the old hall was ever there except the old coach road leading off Moden Hill.

An apparition known as The Grey Lady is said to haunt the whole area around the school and the school itself. She has been seen on the old coach road and also inside the school buildings.

Some years ago, the author was involved in the making of a film about the Grey Lady by sixth formers at Ellowes Hall School in conjunction with Wolverhampton's Lighthouse Film Company. During the filming, the ghost seemed particularly active. Staff at the school reported feeling presences and seeing figures flitting around doorways.

Although the Grey Lady is locally associated with the old Ellowes Hall there is no evidence as to who she might have been or why she haunts the area. One local legend has it that sighting the Grey Lady would warn miners of an impending pit disaster. Yet another that she is the murdered wife of a brutal husband who discovered her in the arms of another man in their bedroom at Ellowes Hall.

The Chapel House
Ruiton Street
Gornal
DY3 2EG

52.522044, -2.123154

The Chapel House was the original name of this pub which is possibly the oldest in Gornal being first licensed in 1834. However, from 1882 until fairly recently it was called The Miners Arms. The Chapel House name derives from local Methodists, known as the Gornal Ranters, who used the back room of the building for their meetings from 1820 despite being staunch teetotallers themselves.

During its time as The Miners Arms the pub played host to a number of strange experiences. A figure has been seen a few times in the pub who simply disappears when he is spotted. He has been known to approach the bar as if to order a drink and then just vanish.

On one occasion, the pub experienced what can only be described as extreme poltergeist type activity. On coming downstairs one morning after hearing nothing during the night the landlord found that all the furniture had been moved and a heavy cabinet pushed against the front door. No sign of forced entry or indeed any intruders at all could be found.

Changing the name back to the Chapel House appears to have done nothing to abate the activity here. When new managers recently took over their CCTV security cameras captured a mop falling over by itself and a 'wet floor' safety sign seemingly folding itself up with no-one anywhere near it.

Old Bulls Head
Redhall Road
Gornal
DY3 2NU

52.517721, -2.126577

Another old Black Country pub with strong connections to the butchery trade is the Old Bulls Head Inn. Licensed in 1834 to Edward Guest, he was a butcher by trade. Many people with existing trades took advantage of Wellington's 1830 Beer Act to take out a beerhouse licence and turn over a room to the sale of beer.

At least three ghosts are said to haunt the Old Bulls Head Inn and the building is subject to poltergeist type activity Objects disappear and reappear again in strange places. On one occasion, a book was taken from the bookcase and left open on the table even though no-one had touched it. It had been in place on the bookshelf just minutes before. A similar thing happened with a beermat whilst the bar was being cleaned. The mat was picked up from the floor and placed on a table. When the cleaner turned around it was on the floor again. This happened not just once but four times.

Figures have been seen walking upstairs and moving around in seemingly empty rooms. The three ghosts reputedly haunting the Old Bulls Head include a man in the cellar, a grey lady and a lady in red who haunts the area behind the pub which may have been a coach house at one time.

The story of the lady in red is an all too familiar one. A servant girl who fell in love with someone above her station and was cruelly jilted after falling pregnant by him. She hung herself from the rafters of the old brewhouse belonging to the pub.

St James the Great
Church Street
Gornal
DY3 2PF

52.519459, -2.124007

Around 1881 the Church of St James the Great in Lower Gornal was the scene of a frightening outbreak of paranormal activity. It all started when the Vicar and local magistrate, Reverend Rooker, was disturbed by voices coming from his back yard one Saturday night. On going to investigate he was shot in the head and left for dead. His assailant was Charles Hartland. Once a member of the choir Hartland had fallen foul of the police and blamed Rooker for his misfortune, swearing to get his revenge. The Reverend was fortunate enough to recover from his injury, but local people began to experience unnerving events around the churchyard. Very quickly alarm spread amongst the God-fearing folk of Gornal.

The ghost of Charles Hartland was seen even though the man was very much alive and in prison for his crimes. Other spectres were seen, and voices heard both in the churchyard and the adjoining field. Phantom figures were also reported flitting around the gravestones and jumping out at people. At the height of the disturbances the choir demanded strong male escorts when practising in the church. Police and a local vigilante group failed to get to the bottom of the strange events although one night they did manage to apprehend both the Reverend himself and one of their own party!

Whatever was going on back in 1881 and for a long time after, it was sufficient to keep most sensible local folk well away from St James's churchyard at night.

The Brittania
Kent Street
Gornal
DY3 1UX

52.527846, -2.116065

The Brittania is nicknamed 'Sallies' after Sallie Williams who ran the quaint old pub until her death in 1991. At that time, it was a pub with no bar and Sallie would serve beer from taps in the wall in her back room. In the mid-1800s the pub was run by a local Sedgley nailmaker, John Jukes, but from 1862 the licensee was Henry Perry who was also a butcher. At this time meat was sold from the front of the building and beer at the rear with a slaughterhouse in the back yard. Beer and butchery were common bedfellows in the Black Country of this period.

Much activity has been experienced here. Dogs seem particularly afraid of the entrance to the cellar and have been known to follow some unseen presence around the lounge. Things often get moved around and sometimes go missing altogether only to turn up in obvious places. The bar has been particularly susceptible to hanging glasses which suddenly start swinging and ornaments being thrown across the room in front of startled customers.

The ladies' toilets are perhaps the most haunted part of the pub. An old lady dressed all in black was seen here by two young girls who fled the building in terror. A more benign spirit is that of a young girl in Victorian clothes with a black and white dog who sits quietly on the window ledge. Female customers have good reason not to visit the toilets alone here.

The Old Mill
Windmill Street
Gornal
DY3 2DQ

52.527739, -2.119474

The Old Mill is named after one of two windmills which existed in Gornal. The public house was originally called The Windmill and after refurbishment is now just The Mill. The remains of one, Ruiton Windmill, can still be seen in nearby Vale Street but the windmill which gave the pub its original name has long since disappeared.

In common with many other Black Country pubs The Mill has a long history of poltergeist type activity. Things get moved around when there is nobody in the pub and unexplained bumps and bangs are often heard. As far as is known no actual apparition has been seen here but this part of Gornal has a history of strange occurrences and paranormal activity.

Back in 1998 the author was part of a paranormal investigation carried out here. Odd bumps and bangs were indeed noted at the time, but one incident was particularly memorable. At one point the relative silence was broken by a loud banging coming from down in the cellar. Typical poltergeist activity we thought. On reaching the bottom of the cellar steps the banging carried on unabated. Until the ice cube machine had finished dropping its contents into a metal bucket that is!

The Woodman
Wakelams Fold
Gornal
DY3 2UD

52.517416, -2.133624

Wakelams Fold is an unusual name for Gornal and is related to the Wakelam family who ran the pub in the mid-1920s and up until the mid-1930s. The Woodman itself is much older and dates back to at least the 1850s.

The pub has been subject to continued poltergeist activity over the years. In the upstairs kitchen, all the plates were once smashed except one which was left in the middle of the floor. A large key went missing only to reappear the following day in the middle of a bed which had only just been made.

Perhaps the most surprising activity here, certainly for the staff and customers who witness it, is full pint glasses being lifted off the bar tables and placed on the floor without a drop being spilt. On one occasion, a heavy metal spirit measure was thrown in the main bar by some unseen hand. Fortunately, it dropped just short of a customer ordering a pint.

Activity in the bar seems to carry on after hours when everyone has gone to bed. Darts are left out or in the board as if a game has been played. The television gets plugged back in after it was unplugged. Occasionally the alarm will go off in the early hours, but no intruder is ever found.

The author was part of an investigation here some years back and during the night voices were heard in the bar area although the source could not be traced. The door to the cellar was found to be locked and when checked again it was unlocked even though no-one had been anywhere near.

Hagley

Hagley War Memorial
60 Park Road
Hagley
DY9 0QF

52.423006, -2.132853

Hagley War Memorial commemorates those brave soldiers who fell in the two World Wars together with more recent conflicts. The cross was dedicated in 1922 but is not in its original position as it was moved 40 yards in 1963 to make way for improvements to the old road.

The island where the A491 Hagley Road to Bromsgrove meets the A456 road to Kidderminster has been the site of some strange experiences. Up until April 2014 a police station was in operation near the island, just off the Kidderminster Road. A police officer had a remarkable encounter whilst on duty here early one morning.

The officer was a very credible witness to what occurred whilst he was out on patrol in the small hours. As he drove his Panda car up towards the island he was surprised to see what he described as a small troop of soldiers walking along by the War Memorial. They were wearing what appeared to be First World War Uniforms. The officer though that they must be re-enactors on their way to an event but given the early hour was intrigued enough to drive around the island in order to have a quick word with them.

By the time he had driven back around the island to get a better look they were nowhere to be seen. The island and the roads leading off it were silent and deserted. What's more, there was nowhere the men could possibly have gone in the short time it took the officer to drive back.

Halesowen

Halesowen Abbey
Manor Way
Halesowen
B62 8RJ

52.443494, -2.036736

Halesowen Abbey was established around 1218 and was home to Cistercians known as 'white canons' due to their wearing of white habits. The Abbey prospered up until 1538 and the dissolution of the monasteries, being partly demolished in 1540. Although the remains of the Abbey are cared for by English Heritage the site is on private land and can only be viewed from a public footpath or on occasional open days.

The 'white lady' ghost said to haunt the Haden Hill area has become inextricably linked with Halesowen Abbey in local legend (see page 24). As with many such legends there are variations, but the basic story remains the same. It is one of a local girl, Elaine or Eleanor of Hayseech Mill, falling in love with a young monk at the Abbey. Such a relationship was strictly forbidden, and they would carry on their illicit liaison on the banks of the River Stour with the monk using a secret tunnel leading from the Abbey.

They decided to elope one night but were betrayed to the Abbot. In one version of the story they were both walled up in the tunnel alive as punishment. However, it seems more likely that the monk would simply have been banished from the area. Elaine though may well have taken the blame for leading the young monk astray and treated far more harshly. Thus, we have the classic tale of the silently sobbing 'white lady' ghost searching in vain for her long-lost lover.

Oldnall Road
Wollescote
Halesowen
B63 2JP

52.453707, -2.094258

Oldnall Road running between Stourbridge and Halesowen seems to have more than its fair share of accidents and near misses including drivers swerving into the verge to avoid someone or something which suddenly appears in the road in front of them.

Although part of the road is in the countryside what the drivers often say they swerve to avoid is no fox or badger. On a number of occasions, the ghost of a child described as being in Victorian style dress has been seen standing in the middle of the road. After swerving to avoid the frightening apparition there is never any sign of a child, or indeed anyone else on this isolated stretch of road.

In some cases, the child is described as being a little girl and in others a boy. One couple who had this unnerving experience were both adamant is was a little Victorian boy they had swerved to avoid.

The same stretch of road has also had sightings of a well-dressed young woman in period clothes standing in the verge and a male figure in black. On nearby Foxcote Lane late one afternoon a retired gentleman braked to avoid knocking down a man in Victorian clothes. He needn't have worried. The man passed straight through the gentleman's car.

Withit Witch
75 (30) High Street
Halesowen
B63 3BQ

52.449710, -2.050491

Halesowen Knitting Centre, rather appropriately named Withit Witch, is reputedly one of the oldest buildings in Halesowen. Together with numbers 31 and 32 it forms a small group of Grade II listed buildings. Number 30 (now renumbered 75) is a timber framed building thought to date back to at least circa 1450.

The building is haunted by a ghost who has come to be called Edward. He makes his presence felt by bringing intense cold with him which is felt by anyone standing near. He also comes with a strong whiff of cigarette smoke which is never seen but only smelt. He has also been known to open and close the doors, move things around and flash the lights on and off especially if there are children in the shop who happen to misbehave.

During a paranormal investigation at the shop some of the reported phenomena was experienced by the author and other members of the team. Whilst in the unused upstairs part of the building one of the shop owners and the author experienced the very strong smell of cigarette smoke which appeared to be just localised in the room we were in. Later on in the investigation odd light effects were noticed and recorded on video in the shop part of the building. This low-level light phenomenon took the form of little flashes which seemed to move around the room. Despite a thorough search, no obvious source for these light anomalies could be found.

Himley

The Crooked House
Coppice Mill
Himley
DY3 4DA

52.515026, -2.152171

The Crooked House, as the name suggests, has suffered from mining subsidence which creates some weird effects in the old part of the pub. Marbles appear to roll uphill on the window ledges but this is nothing paranormal, more a mix of subsidence and optical illusion but entertaining none the less.

Originally built as a farmhouse in 1765 it was once owned by Sir Stephen Glynne, whose sister Catherine was married to Prime Minister Gladstone. The pub was once called The Glynne Arms in recognition of this former owner. Glynne himself was responsible for the coal mining which would one day make the future pub so well known.

The pub is home to at least two ghosts. The first is believed to be a past landlord, a short gentleman in his 60s or 70s, who is seen to enter the old bar and then simply disappear before ordering a drink. Another apparition is known locally as Polly. She haunts the area around the old fireplace dressed as a parlour maid. She may well date back to the time the building was a farmhouse before it became a pub.

The fields behind the pub are also subject to paranormal activity in the form of a group of children playing together. Little notice would be taken of them except for the fact that their clothes date to a much earlier time.

The Dudley Arms
Wolverhampton Road
Himley
DY3 4LB

52.519555, -2.175757

The name Dudley Arms reflects the fact that the pub was once owned by the Earl of Dudley whose family seat was nearby Himley Hall. It was subsequently purchased by the Wolverhampton and Dudley Breweries Ltd in 1929. The pub also has a connection with Edward, Prince of Wales, before he was crowned Edward VIII in 1936.

Prince Edward was very good friends with William Humble Eric Ward, 3rd Earl of Dudley, and often visited Himley Hall sometimes accompanied by his future wife, Wallace Simpson. On one very memorable occasion for all concerned, Edward and Eric Ward paid an impromptu visit to the Dudley Arms and bought everyone present a drink.

It is no real surprise that The Dudley Arms is haunted given the amount of paranormal activity reported in the surrounding area. The pub has long been subject to fairly low-level poltergeist type activity which is more of an annoyance to staff rather than anything more sinister.

The source of this activity is said to be one of the previous landlords. He loved the pub so much he simply refuses to leave. Staff know when he is present because lights often get switched back on again both upstairs and downstairs in the bar areas. They can be certain that lights have been turned off after closing up for the night only to find them turned back on again either very soon after or the following morning. It seems that this particular ghost is none too keen on the dark!

Himley Hall
Himley Road
Himley
DY3 4DF

52.521905, -2.166150

Once owned by the Earls of Dudley, Himley Hall is popular with people looking to enjoy the parkland surrounding the Palladian mansion. But after dark, once the wrought iron gates are locked, the park takes on a far more sinister atmosphere.

Stories of ghostly cavaliers are common in and around the Black Country which was heavily embroiled in the Civil War. In this case, however, there is a contemporary record as to how and why a soldier of King Charles I met his death in the grounds of Himley Hall.

This record comes from a diary written by Richard Symonds who accompanied the Royalist army on its marches. Symond's diary records that on Friday 16th May 1645, the Royalist army commanded by Charles I camped for just one night in the grounds of Himley Hall. They were en route to the ill-fated battle of Naseby. He goes on to further report that, 'one soldjer was hanged for mutiny' after trying to desert whilst they were camped at Himley. The unfortunate man was captured trying to get away and tried on the spot. Justice was swift in those days and the soldier was hanged from a suitable tree and buried in the grounds before the army departed.

His unquiet spirit is said to wander the park at night and has been witnessed a number of times. A small number of permits are available for all night fishing in the Great Pool at Himley Hall. On occasions, fishermen have realised they are not alone when suddenly startled by a figure described as an 'old fashioned soldier' moving silently through the trees.

Himley Road
Himley Park
Himley
DY3 4LA

52.518552, -2.166592

The Himley Road, where it runs alongside the grounds of Himley Hall near the entrance to Home Farm, has for a long time been subject to mysterious sightings. On numerous occasions motorists have had to brake hard when a figure dashes across the road straight in front of them.

On her way home to Sedgley one dark November evening, secretary Diane Johnson had an experience she will never forget. Having driven a short way along the Himley Road she was startled by a figure which ran straight in front of the car. It all happened too quickly for Diane to discern any details of the figure except that she was certain he was wearing long cavalier style boots. Where he passed in front of the car is a very long, tall fence which borders Himley Hall. This may well be the same cavalier who is said to haunt Himley Hall itself (see page 62). There is no gap in the fence here where the figure could have passed through. Diane is not the only motorist to have been startled by spectral figures from the past along this exact stretch of road.

Yet another apparition has been seen crossing the Himley Road at the same spot immediately outside the hall. This ghost is also seen in the hall itself but very little is known about her. She appears to be a servant girl judging by her long, plain dress and is usually seen on the upper floors of the hall. She is seemingly oblivious to any traffic and disappears through the high wooden fence which surrounds the park.

Right at the place where these apparitions pass through the fence there used to be an old iron gate leading directly into the grounds of Himley Hall.

Holbeche House
Wolverhampton Road
Himley
DY6 7DA

52.512257, -2.171362

Holbeche House is now a private care home but back in 1605 it was the scene of a bloody battle between the remaining Gun Powder Plotters and the Sheriff of Worcestershire's men. The Plotters had replenished their stock of gunpowder at Hewell Grange but had got it wet on the way to Holbeche House, owned by Stephen Lyttleton. In drying the powder by an open fire, it was accidentally ignited, and the ensuing blast had alerted the Sheriff's men who mounted a siege. The Plotters that weren't killed were captured and later executed thus ending the Gunpowder Plot.

It is hardly surprising that a building steeped in such a violent history should harbour a ghost or two. A young groom, Gideon Grove, who tried to escape the melee at Holbeche is said to haunt the Bridgnorth Road in nearby Wombourne (see story on page 166).

Another apparition at Holbeche appears in a long, dark cloak and wearing a tall pointed hat. He has been seen in various parts of the old building but especially in and around the main staircase in the entrance hall.

The author was part of a paranormal investigation at Holbeche House some years ago and this dark, shadowy figure was seen to pass under the staircase and emerge in a corridor on the other side. Investigators on both sides saw this figure pass through. A video camera set up facing the stairs should have captured the whole event but failed to record anything. Strangely, it was working perfectly before and after the event.

Spring Heeled Jack
Wolverhampton Road
Himley
DY3 4LD

52.519000, -2.175333

In the middle 1800s the Black Country was plagued with stories of a figure with glowing red eyes, cloven hooves and horns leaping across buildings and often leaving hoof prints on the roofs. This was the legendary Spring Heeled Jack. There were reports from right across the Black Country including Netherton in 1877.

There were multiple witnesses to Spring Heeled Jack leaping across the canal in dead of night with one bright shining eye. The local constabulary showing great resolve surrounded and managed to capture what they naturally assumed was Spring Heeled Jack. Only to find they had actually captured champion jumper, Joe Darby, practising his standing jumps over the canal in the dark wearing a miner's lamp!

However, one of the most confirmed sightings of Spring Heeled Jack himself occurred at Himley not far from the Himley House Hotel also in 1877. The Dudley Militia were deployed to apprehend the fiend but, unlike the Netherton constabulary, proved grossly inadequate when Spring Heeled Jack suddenly loomed out of the darkness at them and could be heard laughing maniacally as the militia to a man ran away! A local farmer proved to be of slightly sterner stuff and he at least managed to fire a shot at Spring Heeled Jack, but it exploded harmlessly in a ball of flame. Only a circle of scorched grass remained as evidence of the farmer's self-professed bravado!

Kinver

Drakelow
Kingsford Lane
Near Kinver
DY11 5SW

52.428023, -2.262250

On a dark winter's night Drakelow Lane leading to Kingsford Lane can be a mysterious place and certainly not somewhere you would want to break down. Drakelow or 'dracan hlaw' in Anglo Saxon refers to a 'Dragons Mound', hill or burial ground. The whole area surrounding Drakelow is subject to many reports of paranormal phenomena.

Apart from the nearby Drakelow Tunnel's nuclear bunker which itself is haunted (see page 67), strange figures have also been seen crossing the lane. A particularly bizarre sighting of these figures came to light whilst the author was following up an unrelated story.

The family concerned were driving home along Drakelow Lane late one November night and had just passed the nuclear bunker on the right. Caught in the car headlights the driver, his wife and daughter clearly saw three figures appear to drift across the road approximately fifteen feet up in the air.

To the witnesses the figures appeared to be solid and were assumed to be monks as they were hooded and dressed in dark brown or black habits. They seemed to be surrounded by some sort of light mist as they floated across. The sighting lasted a good few seconds as the apparitions drifted out of the trees right in front of the car. It is possible that the figures weren't monks.

Drakelow is an ancient place and in Celtic belief the Genii Cucullati were guardian spirits, especially of holy places such as burial mounds. They have the appearance of hooded monks. And there are almost always three of them.

Drakelow Tunnels
Kingsford Lane
Near Kinver
DY11 5SW

52.427207, -2.265497

Drakelow Tunnels began life as a shadow factory for British Leyland during World War II producing aero engines. During the Cold War, it became a nuclear bomb shelter designated as Regional Seat of Government 9 (RSG9). It is possible to visit the tunnels at times and the whole complex is hopefully going to be turned into a museum.

The tunnels were originally dug out of sandstone. Explosives were used to blast out over 3 miles of this underground complex, and not without serious accidents. One of the worst happened in October 1941, when a roof fall in Tunnel 1 claimed the lives of three men including Harry Depper.

In the tunnel's themselves 1940's wartime music has sometimes been heard seemingly coming from Tunnel 1. When the source of the music is investigated it abruptly stops. Strange mists have also been seen particularly in and around Tunnel 4. On one occasion, a caretaker's two German Shepherds were transfixed by a misty figure in this Tunnel. The dogs ran off terrified and would not return. People often experience the feeling of being watched and some claim to have been touched or even pushed. A male figure has been seen and on one occasion disappearing around a fully lit doorway. This figure has been given the name 'Oswald' and is purported to have been one of the workers killed during the construction of the tunnels.

On a recent investigation attended by the author a tremendous bang was heard and recorded in 1st Avenue, Government Department, near one of the nuclear blast doors. There was no-one anywhere near the area concerned and a thorough search revealed no clue as to what might have happened.

Dunsley Hall
39 Dunsley Road
Kinver
DY7 6LU

52.455764, -2.210077

Historic Dunsley Hall is a Grade II listed, late 16th century building which these days is a charming country hotel. From 1709 the house was owned by the wealthy Foley family who held it as part of the Prestwood Estate until selling it to Alfred Marsh of Marsh and Baxter Limited in 1918.

In years past the house had connections with the brutal murder of farmer Benjamin Robins of Dunsley Hall by notorious William Howe in 1812. The ghost of William Howe is said to haunt Gibbet Lane (see page 69).

Whether the murdered Benjamin Robins is one of the ghosts haunting Dunsley Hall is not known. However, staff and guests have had paranormal experiences at the hotel. On occasions, a ghostly figure has been seen at the bar and the quiet lady who is sometimes passed on the stairs is no physical guest or member of staff. A gentleman has also been seen sitting in the lounge in the early mornings only to disappear when the staff go to take his order.

Poltergeist type activity is also experienced here with things disappearing only to reappear in some obvious place. Staff and guests have also been known to get locked in the bedrooms. When this happens, the key is invariably discovered on the outside of the door.

Gibbet Lane
Kinver
Stourbridge
DY7 6PX

52.453261, -2.179954

On December 18th 1812 farmer Benjamin Robins was returning home on foot from a successful day at Stourbridge market. He was unfortunate enough to meet up with William Howe who had just two things on his mind, robbery and murder. Shooting Benjamin Robins at close range with a pistol, Howe robbed the unfortunate man and left him for dead. But Robins did not die, at least not immediately, and managed to stagger back home to Dunsley Hall. Robins died of his wound ten days later, on December 28th. Such was the level of outrage at the murder that Bow Street Runners were employed to ensure the culprit was brought to justice.

Howe was eventually apprehended following an investigation by the Bow Street Runners. He was duly sentenced and hanged at Stafford Gaol. Howe had the dubious distinction of being one of the last men in England to be 'gibbeted' or hung in chains at the site of the murder as a warning to others.

Since then the ghost of William Howe is said to haunt Gibbet Lane. Dark, shadowy figures have been seen and the sounds of clanking chains heard. A gentleman in 1872 was confronted by the terrifying spectre and lashed out with his stick. The stick passed right through and knocked the gentleman off his feet. Howe raised his arms and with a menacing chuckle faded away.

There are reports of people being followed including one from 1940 when a lady was stalked in the moonlight by a figure with a long neck which she said appeared to be broken. He made no sound and cast no shadow. Fortunately for the lady concerned the apparition disappeared as soon as she passed the place where Howe's body had been gibbeted.

Phantom Highwayman
Stourbridge Road
Kinver
DY7 6LU

52.451150, -2.206429

The stretch of road between The Manor House of Whittington and the traffic lights at Stourton on the A449 is said to be haunted by the ghost of a notorious highwayman. He wears a tricorn hat and with pistol in hand rides a magnificent horse. There have been a number of sightings of Captain Kitson over the years galloping hell-for-leather in the nearby fields and charging across the road in front of astonished motorists.

One such credible witness to the phantom highwayman was a nurse in the early 1990s. She was making her way back home in the early hours of the morning after a late-night shift. As she drove along the road towards Stourton she became aware of movement in the field to her left. Something seemed to be keeping pace with her car. All of a sudden, a horse and rider leapt over the hedge and galloped straight in front of her car. Fearing an unavoidable collision with man and horse she slammed on the brakes and the car slewed into the verge. But there was no collision. The road was empty and quiet with no sign of the horse or the mysterious rider. In giving a description of the dangerous rider later that morning to the local police she was adamant that the man she saw was wearing a tricorn hat and was carrying a pistol. There is no telling what the police officer made of her strange experience.

The Whittingham Inn
Whittington
Kinver
DY7 6NY

52.443336, -2.211930

The Whittington Inn is now known as The Manor House of Whittington. Whittington Manor dates back to 1310 and was built by Sir William De Whittington as a hunting lodge. It is possible that Richard Whittington stayed here at least for a time before seeking his fortune in London as 'Dick Whittington'.

The building has historic ties with royalty. The young Lady Jane Grey is said to have stayed here, as did Charles II during his flight after the battle of Worcester. Queen Anne stayed in 1711 and bestowed the house with her royal seal. During the Reformation, Catholic Priests and sympathisers made good use of the priest holes hidden within the walls.

With such an impressive history, it would be reasonable to expect the building to harbour a ghost or two and indeed it does. One of the ghosts seen here is described as a monk. Given that the building has several priest holes it is likely that he was given refuge here, no doubt in terror of being found.

The other significant ghost is said to be that of Lady Jane Grey who is thought to have stayed in the original manor house. Her apparition is seen dressed in a pale coloured, long flowing dress. Although she has been seen in various parts of the pub she is known to sweep down the staircase into the main bar area where she promptly disappears. The discovery of Elizabethan wall paintings a few years ago increased activity with objects being moved and footsteps heard. This culminated in the Assistant Manager at the time seeing the figure of a lady in a long pale dress gliding in front of the bar before fading away on the staircase.

Netherton

Netherton Canal Tunnel
Windmill End
Netherton
DY2 9HU

52.491989, -2.070022

Netherton Canal Tunnel was opened in 1858 and as such was the last canal tunnel to be completed in Britain. Even so, tunnelling was still a dangerous business and eight workmen lost their lives digging this one. It was built to provide a connection between Netherton and Tipton and ease the lengthy queues of barges waiting to use the narrower Dudley Canal Tunnel (see page 30). It is slightly unusual in that it has towpaths on both sides and is wide enough for canal boats to pass inside.

The tunnel also has a long history of haunting. At least two ghosts have been reported here. The first is an old-time policeman who is said to have been murdered in the tunnel. The second is a lady in a dirty white dress, known locally as the 'Grey Lady'.

As well as these apparitions being seen, wet footprints have also been spotted in torchlight leading into the tunnel. If these footprints are followed they suddenly disappear deep inside with no clue as to who, or what, made them. People walking through the darkness of the tunnel have also heard what they assume is someone in heavy boots approaching them from behind. On turning around the footsteps immediately stop and there is no-one to be seen. Perhaps the boots belong to the old-style policeman, or even to one of those Victorian workmen who met their untimely deaths in here.

Oldbury

Rood End Cemetery
St Paul's Road
Oldbury
B66 1QT

52.499167, -1.992833

Rood End Cemetery was established by the Oldbury Burial Board in 1857. By the 1930s the cemetery was attracting a good deal of interest for the regular appearance of strange lights emanating from the gravestones at night. This phenomenon has been witnessed on numerous occasions and even to this day stories of the glowing headstones persist. Those brave enough to approach the headstones usually report that the glowing gradually disappears as they get nearer.

Whilst this is certainly a strange phenomenon, there are a few other reliable reports of similar glowing gravestones particularly in America. A good example is Forest Hill Cemetery just east of Evart in Michigan. As is the case at Rood End no satisfactory explanation has yet been found for the strangely glowing headstones. One interesting feature that reports seem to share is that the lights are seen clearly from a distance but begin to fade away as they are approached as is the case with the Rood End lights.

There has naturally been a lot of speculation about the cause of the strange light effects including nearby street lights, reflections from the moon and even naturally occurring bioluminescence. Reflections seem unlikely as it has been reported that even non-reflective gravestones have been seen to glow in perfectly dry conditions. So, is it paranormal? Possibly not, but rather a strange mystery none the less.

The Barley Mow
City Road
Oldbury
B69 1QS

52.505629, -2.044156

The Barley Mow is no longer in existence and the land has now been used for a small housing development. As far as is known the paranormal activity ceased when the pub was demolished. However, the original pub is available in Google Past Street View for September 2007.

The pub used to experience a range of paranormal activity including the smell of toast burning early in the morning even though no-one had been toasting bread. The beer would also go flat on occasions for no apparent reason which the staff took to signify that an increase in ghostly activity was sure to follow.

Shadowy figures would often be seen flitting through the pub and the ghost of one of the old regulars was a frequent visitor. Sam Cole was a coal man and would often leave his horse and cart outside while he enjoyed a pint or two. The sound of old Sam Cole's horse and cart was often heard in the road outside the pub. Paranormal investigator, George Gregg, was witness to this early one morning when he clearly heard the sound of a horse and cart outside the pub. Not knowing the story of Sam Cole, George had no reason to go and investigate!

Oldswinford

Oldswinford Cross
Oldswinford
DY6 8AA

52.448765, -2.138346

Oldswinford Cross is often busy with drivers leaving Stourbridge Junction train station and people heading out of Stourbridge itself in the direction of Hagley. Not long ago, a lady driver making her way up Glasshouse Hill towards Oldswinford Cross witnessed something she would never forget.

Driving in busy traffic she saw a young girl dressed in what may have been a smock come flying across the road in front of the cars ahead of her. Fearing a terrible accident as she reached the top of the hill she was amazed to see that all was normal. No sign of an accident, no little girl and everything moving along through the traffic lights by the pub just as it should.

There is a triangle formed between Oldswinford, Hagley and Halesowen where sightings of a little girl in old fashioned clothes have been reported either at the side of the road or in the road itself. Such sightings have occurred in the vicinity of the Badger's Sett public house (see page 99) and particularly on Oldnall Road leading towards Halesowen (see page 58) from the direction of Oldswinford. These days Oldswinford is just a small part of Stourbridge but in years past it was a large and important parish in its own right

These sightings might all be related. The apparition seen could well be the same little poor girl, a playback from a far harsher time, making her way along the roads as she did in life, perhaps seeking work and some small comfort.

The Crabmill
Hagley Road
Oldswinford
DY8 2JP

52.445683, -2.139539

The present day Crabmill started life as a private Georgian residence called Thornleigh. The licence from the original Crabmill was transferred in 1970 and the earlier pub demolished. The name Crabmill is most likely a reference to an old cider mill which stood nearby in Oldswinford. In fact, for a while the pub was known as The Oldswinford.

The haunting here seems to have more to do with the private house rather than the later pub. New managers particularly can often look forward to disturbed nights due to the loud movement noises coming from rooms which are known to be empty. They are also likely to be welcomed by a full range of paranormal disturbances including poltergeist activity such as plates being hurled off shelves in the kitchen. Something here doesn't like change.

The apparition of an old gentleman is also seen here. Wearing a top hat and a black coat he has been witnessed by both staff and customers striding purposefully through the pub. Once seen, he disappears just as quickly as he arrived. Locally, this apparition is said to be an old Doctor who allegedly committed suicide in the house. A Doctor Kirkpatrick did live at Thornleigh with his family. He was a prominent local figure and in charge of the military hospital at Wordsley during the First World War. But he certainly didn't commit suicide in the house.

The apparition here could well be a former resident of Thornleigh House. Perhaps he is somewhat perturbed at his old home being turned into a public house or he might just like to keep a watchful eye on his former residence.

Penn

Graseley Old Hall
Carlton Road
Penn Fields
WV3 0LP

52.573769, -2.141253

Graseley Old Hall is Grade II listed and one of the oldest buildings in the area dating back to the 15th Century. Nowadays it is privately owned and not normally open to the public. Back in 2002 the property gained a fair amount of publicity, including television coverage, for being 'The house that cries'. This referred to the random appearance of water dripping from one of the beams in the main hall.

On one occasion, the owner was witness to this and was able to make a thorough check of the rooms above to ensure there was no leakage of water from anywhere. There wasn't. What's more, on returning to the main hall everything was dry. Such occurrences have often been associated with cases of low level poltergeist activity. And it seems there may be some history of this. Owned by the Royal Wolverhampton School from 1930 onwards it was rumoured locally to have suffered sporadic outbreaks of poltergeist activity.

In August 2016, the author was part of a paranormal investigation at the hall. Whilst there was no sign of any anomalous pools of water, footsteps were clearly heard on the stairs and in empty rooms during the night. No explanation could be found for these footsteps at the time they occurred.

Subsequent research revealed that the building was originally built using old ship's timbers. Whether this contributed to the anomalous dripping is of course open to speculation, but nobody whether or not the water was salty!

The Old Stags Head
Pennwood Lane
Penn
WV4 5JB

52.554799, -2.156170

The whole area around The Old Stags Head is steeped in history. A Saxon cross was discovered next to nearby Saint Bartholomew's Church in 1912. The cross is associated with Leofric, the Earl of Mercia. His wife owned Lower Penn, but Lady Godiva is better known for riding naked through the streets of Coventry.

The principal haunting at The Old Stags Head is directly connected with Saint Bartholomew's Church. Going back to Victorian times one of the vicars knew the location of a tunnel leading from the church to the pub cellar. He would make use of it to enjoy regular pints of beer much to the annoyance of his wife. His less than amused wife would follow him through the tunnel into the pub cellar and turn the beer taps off to thwart her husband.

It seems the vicar's wife is still up to her old tricks as the beer taps are sometimes found to be turned off for no apparent reason. The cellar takes on a most strange atmosphere at times. Apparitions of two ladies have been seen in the pub. One rather sombre figure wearing black mourning clothes has been seen in and around the bedrooms, but the most frequent sighting is that of a Victorian lady dressed in white who appears in the bar area. Perhaps she is the vicar's wife hoping to catch her errant husband who has been known to push staff and customers out of the way presumably to avoid her.

Sedgley

Beacon Hotel
Bilston Street
Sedgley
DY3 1JE

52.543588, -2.114429

The Beacon Hotel is a Grade II listed Victorian style pub and home to the Sarah Hughes Brewery. The pub was built around 1851 and has its own tower brewery which is still in use. The building reflects its Victorian origins very much, both in décor and atmosphere.

Sarah Hughes took over the pub in 1921 but by all accounts, still keeps a watchful eye over the pub and not just from her realistic portrait. She was seen by one of the previous managers walking through a wall in the smoke room where there was once a door. Listen carefully in the hallway and you may hear the sounds of someone walking about upstairs and moving things around even though this part of the building is only used for storage.

In 1994 a member of staff, Andy, was staying at the pub for extra security and sleeping in the sitting room. He awoke in the early hours of the morning to see a man standing in the corner of the room. He was an older man dressed in dark trousers, a grandad style shirt, waistcoat and wellington boots. Realising it was a ghost Andy closed his eyes tight and was extremely relieved when he opened them again to see that the figure had vanished. In describing the figure later, it turned out to have been the late father of the present owner.

More recently, the large heavy key used to secure the internal doors went missing from its usual place one night after locking up. A thorough search failed to reveal the whereabouts of the key. It reappeared behind the bar with a loud clatter the following day as if thrown by some invisible hand.

Clifton Cinema
Bull Ring
Sedgley
DY3 1RX

52.541390, -2.122475

The former Clifton Cinema is nowadays a Wetherspoon's pub but still clearly recognisable for what it once was. The Art Deco inspired cinema opened its doors in May 1937. It got its name from the head of the Clifton cinema chain, Captain Sydney Clift. The cinema closed its doors in June 1978 becoming a bingo club until bought by Wetherspoons. The auditorium is still intact but no longer accessible to the public.

The building has long been subject to paranormal activity. A little girl is known to run around the kitchen at night and follow individual members of staff. The kitchen floor gets cleaned last thing at night and on one occasion a single child's footprint was discovered on the previously mopped floor. Frequently after closing, the hand driers can be heard to operate together with bumps and bangs from both the toilet area and the closed off cinema auditorium upstairs.

Janene Hall was employed in the pub a few years back and confirms the strange experiences here including doors banging after time and footsteps following her from the cellar to the bottle store, "Sometimes they would continue after I stopped walking, always out of time to my own". One night when Janine was alone in the cellar a two-inch wooden barrel peg was thrown at her, hitting her squarely in the back. She spun around fully expecting to see someone, but there was nobody there and the cellar door was still closed.

There is a picture in the pub which appears to move if glimpsed in one of the mirrors. Most likely this is simply an optical illusion but then again, the picture is that of a little girl.

Sedgley Police Station
Vicar Street
Sedgley
DY3 3SD

52.540167, -2.123667

Parts of the building that houses Sedgley Police Station date back as far as 1734. It was originally the old parish poor or workhouse housing some sixty inmates. It closed in 1858 by which time it had been replaced by the much larger Dudley Union Workhouse in Upper Gornal. The building was rebuilt and converted to the local police station in the early 1860s.

One of the older police officers who used to be stationed at Sedgley had a most unnerving experience there whilst on night duty. He was on his own in the station and having a sandwich in the kitchen area. Silently and without any warning, a uniformed figure suddenly walked straight past him through the kitchen. The figure came from the direction of the old police inspector's house on the same site. and disappeared through the other side of the kitchen.

According to the officer, the figure was dressed in some sort of uniform and at the time assumed him to be a Victorian police inspector. However, there is a possibility that the figure may have been walking through the earlier workhouse building.

The officer would probably not have known that workhouses such as Sedgley would have employed a porter to oversee all comings and goings, secure the building at night and assist the Master and Matron in keeping the inmates in order. This gentleman would have been identified by his smart, formal, and almost military style of uniform.

The Crown
High Street
Sedgley
DY3 1RJ

52.544300, -2.122167

The current building is relatively new having replaced a much earlier Crown public house on the same site. The haunting of The Crown is associated with a much earlier and rather rotund landlord known as Bob Foster. The story goes that he died suddenly from a massive heart attack whilst working down in the cellar.

Dogs are prone to behaving strangely when Bob is about and often seem to be frightened of something that can't be seen by anyone else present. On one occasion, a previous landlord found himself locked in his own bedroom even though he was on his own in the building at the time.

One of the cleaners claims to have seen Bob in the area around the toilets but he seems to make his presence felt mainly in the cellar where barrels can be heard being moved around when there is no one down there. On one occasion, two draymen delivering barrels of beer were getting rather fed up with the landlord who insisted on barking instructions to them and trying to tell them their job.

They both had the shock of their lives when they were told the man who had been ordering them around down in the cellar was none other than the long-deceased Bob Foster.

Turls Hill Bridleway
Turls Hill
Sedgley
WV14 9HH

52.540774, -2.106178

The area around the Turls Hill Bridleway leading from Sedgley towards Coseley has long been known locally as a somewhat mysterious place. Some of this air of mystery may date back to the First World War when Belgian refugees were housed in the long demolished Turls Hill House. The house became known locally as 'The Belgians' or 'The Belgian Yard'. Most Belgian refugees returned to Belgium after the war.

It is not known whether the ghost who haunts the bridleway is associated with Turls Hill House or not. People who have seen her describe a veiled lady dressed in white moving through the trees. Local legend has it that on separate occasions her two sons committed suicide by shooting themselves in a nearby quarry.

A former industrialist owner of Turls Hill House is also reputed to have committed suicide by shooting himself in the quarry after going bankrupt. It seems to be quite a coincidence that three suicides by shooting should have taken place in the same quarry. If there is any truth in these suicide stories at all perhaps local legend has confused them over the years. If so, the veiled lady could be wandering Turls Hill either searching for her lost boys or else her suicidal husband.

White Lion Inn
Bilston Street
Sedgley
DY3 1JF

52.543264, -2.115530

The White Lion Inn certainly dates to at least 1702 but parts of it are reputed to go back to the time of the English Civil War. Dudley was a Royalist stronghold during the Civil War and this may account for one of the ghosts seen here.

He is a Royalist Cavalier in full uniform who has been seen in various parts of the building but particularly on the main staircase. Dudley Castle is not far away so he may have been associated with the forces who defended the castle against the Parliamentarians. At that time, the castle was actually part of Sedgley with a much later border change placing it in Dudley in 1926.

A slightly more recent apparition is that of an old lady who has been seen in various parts of the pub. She is locally known as Ann, the wife of a former licensee. Before the pub was refurbished there used to be a little window in the kitchen door leading from the bar. The ghost of Ann was often to be seen keeping watch over the pub from this window. Ann used to enjoy a glass of gin and at times the gin optic has been heard being operated when the bar is empty.

With most ghostly sightings, the apparition usually behaves as they would have done in life even though they may pass through non-existent doors or walk above or below modern floor levels. An apparition has been seen in The White Lion who does not conform to these ghostly conventions. A man in normal clothes is seen to walk in the pub as if to buy a drink. Before reaching the bar, he starts to float up in the air and disappears through the ceiling!

Shropshire (east)

Boscobel House
Bishop's Wood
Shropshire
ST19 9AR

52.67201, -2.242039

Boscobel House dates back to 1632 and was a hunting lodge and a Catholic safe house with its priest holes, one of which was used by Charles II after his defeat at the battle of Worcester in 1651. It was here that Charles really did successfully hide from Parliamentarian soldiers in an Oak tree accompanied by a Major Careless. Fortunately for Charles the Major did not live up to his name and they remained undetected.

From here Charles was taken to Moseley Old Hall (see page 157). However, it does not appear to be Charles himself who haunts this beautiful old building. Disembodied voices have been heard in the building especially around the area of the White Room. On one occasion, the Custodian's son, in the room on his own, was startled by someone clearly saying, "Do you remember me?".

On another occasion, a visitor on one of the guided tours saw the apparition of a lady in what she described as 'a white swirly dress' coming down the stairs from the attic. She mentioned briefly seeing the swish of the lady's petticoat as she descended the steep stairs before disappearing. No-one had been upstairs in the attic at the time of the sighting. The building belongs to English Heritage and it is well worth taking a guided tour. Who knows what you may experience here?

Madam Pigott
Chetwynd
Shropshire
TF10 8AD

52.788861, -2.392960

Chetwynd Hall was demolished in the 1960s. The ghost story here concerns Madam Pigott, the young wife of Squire Pigott who had married her only to ensure an heir to inherit his estate. He cared little for his new wife and spent most of his time in London frequenting houses of ill repute and drinking establishments. Madam Pigott was left alone and bitter with her health suffering, especially when she became pregnant.

The birth was a difficult one for both mother and child and Squire Pigott was asked by the Doctor to choose between his wife and baby. Without hesitation, he chose the baby. With Madam Pigott's dying breath, she put a curse on the Squire. The baby fared no better and did not survive very long.

It was not long before the troublesome spirit of Madam Pigott was making her presence felt. Her weeping apparition was seen to wander the grounds of Chetwynd Hall clutching her baby. She would sit on the twisted roots of an old tree and terrify anyone who came near. Twelve Clergymen were employed to trap her spirit in a bottle and cast it into Chetwynd Pool. A particularly harsh winter iced over the pool and cracked the bottle. Madam Pigott was out and more frightening than ever.

Her ghost was said to have jumped in the saddles of passing horses behind their terrified male riders. Twelve Clergymen were again employed to contain her but to seemingly no avail as Madam Pigott still haunts the area. In more recent times she has appeared around Chetwynd Church and the A41 road to Newport. A figure wearing a white dress and holding a baby has been seen wandering around forlornly or sitting at the side of the road weeping.

Naughty Nells
Market Place
Shifnal
TF11 9BA

52.665331, -2.372633

aughty Nells was closed at the time of writing. It was originally called The Unicorn and was a busy stopover point for the many London stagecoaches which passed through during the 18th century. The Grade II listed building has been associated with one of the mistresses of Charles II, the actress Nell Gwynne. Charles certainly had local connections after escaping the battle of Worcester and hiding just up the road at Boscobel House and Moseley Old Hall. Indeed, Nell herself may have been born in Herefordshire. However, the Nell associated with Shifnal is more likely to be one of Charles Dickens's characters, Nell Trent or 'Little Nell' of Old Curiosity Shop fame. Dickens certainly visited Shifnal on a number of occasions as his grandmother was said to have worked at Tong Castle.

The building is said to be haunted by at least four ghosts. They manifest themselves through disembodied voices and loud banging noises coming from locked and empty rooms as though people were trying to get out. Shifnal suffered a great fire in 1591 and whilst the building was not destroyed it is easy to imagine people desperate to escape the smoke and flames.

If you visit Shifnal be sure to have a close look at the upstairs bedroom windows. Even though Naughty Nells is closed and empty you might just see an expressionless face staring right back at you.

Royal Airforce Museum
Cosford
Shropshire
TF11 8UP

52.644411, -2.313434

The Warplanes Hangar at The Royal Airforce Museum, Cosford is said to be actively haunted especially around the Lincoln Bomber exhibit. Avro Lincoln RF398 is known as Cosford's 'Haunted Bomber'. The Lincoln was heavily based on the famous Lancaster heavy bomber of World War II 'Dambusters' fame but the Lincoln at Cosford was never used operationally during the war.

In 1991, BBC presenter Gwyn Richards and paranormal investigator Ivan Spenceley made overnight recordings from inside the bomber which sounded like switches were being thrown even though they were alone in the aircraft. There are also reports of an airman in full flying dress seen in the hangar and a helmeted figure in the aeroplane itself. One of the engineers restoring the plane was working on his own in the hanger when he dropped a spanner. Imagine his surprise when the spanner was handed straight back to him!

Whilst locking up one night a misty figure was seen in the hanger and a secretary had her name clearly called whilst alone and pinning notes to a noticeboard. She refused to ever go in there alone again. An electrician who fell from 15 feet up should have been injured but said his fall was broken as he was 'caught' by something before hitting the ground.

Legend has it that Master Pilot Hiller was the last person to fly the plane and always said he would haunt 'his baby'. He was allegedly killed in an air crash at Cosford in 1963. Reason enough for the bomber to be haunted. However, detailed records are kept of aircraft and the last person to fly RF398 was Flt Lt John Langley. Not only that but there is no record that a Master Pilot Hiller ever existed let alone that he was killed in an air crash at Cosford.

The Anvil Inn
22 Aston Road
Shifnal
TF11 8DU

52.667326, -2.368451

The Anvil Inn dates back to at least 1701 but may be even earlier. In the days when the London stagecoaches stopped off in Shifnal, wagon wheels were repaired in the wainwrights opposite. The old blacksmith's anvil, which is still there, is how the pub got its name.

The old inn has an extra ghostly member of staff who has been seen walking behind the bar. The apparition has been seen fleetingly in the large mirror which hangs over the fireplace. People also see movement out of the corner of their eye behind the bar when there is no-one there. Tantalisingly, who or what the figure is can never quite be discerned.

The cellar has quite a strange feeling of someone watching. And indeed, there may well be someone watching over the pub. Over a period of some time there were problems with one of the gas bottles. It was used to pump soft drinks up to the bar. It would be turned on at opening time only to find shortly after that the tap would be turned off again even though no-one had been in the cellar. It got to be so bad that a gas engineer was called in.

As soon as he entered the cellar the engineer said there was indeed a serious problem, but it wasn't with the gas bottle. Mains gas had been slowly leaking into the cellar from a loose joint in the supply pipe. It had been so gradual that the staff hadn't noticed. If it had been left, with all the electrical equipment in the cellar, there could eventually have been a major catastrophe.

The strange thing was, once the leak had been repaired there was no further trouble with the gas bottle.

The Bell Inn
Newport Road
Tong
TF11 8PS

52.670100, -2.309608

The new Bell Inn opened in 1828 to replace the old Bell Inn which became a farm house. It was built on the site of a medieval wayside cross which had been replaced by an 18th century obelisk milestone. The 19th century country public house has a large conservatory which is used as an extra dining room.

It is here in the conservatory that the ghost of a mischievous little girl is seen flitting amongst the tables. She is only ever seen for a split second and often only out the corner of the eye, but the description of the little girl is always the same. She has long, curly hair and is seen wearing a party dress.

The little girl is also prone to rearranging the cutlery. After tables have been laid ready for diners and whilst the room is empty the cutlery gets moved in a very particular way. She likes nothing better than to cross the knives and forks over at right angles to each other.

On occasions, the staff have laid the tables the night before ready for the following day before locking up. They open up again the following morning, only to find all the cutlery in the conservatory neatly crossed over.

The Horns of Boningale
Holyhead Road
Albrighton
WV7 3DA

52.621615, -2.274400

The Horns of Boningale has a history going back some three hundred years. It used to offer basic food and accommodation to Shropshire drovers who would pen up their sheep overnight whilst waiting for Staffordshire drovers to take over en route to Wolverhampton.

The drovers stayed in a bunkhouse which has now become the dining room. The story goes that a fight between two drovers resulted in the death of one of them. Since then, the apparition of a man dressed in a smock has been seen in the dining room usually leaning up against the mantlepiece.

One ghost even helps with the cleaning! One of the previous managers encountered her early one morning. On coming up from the cellar after a delivery she was amazed to see a short lady busy cleaning the tables in the dining room to her left. Her own cleaner was in the bar to her right and had seen nothing. By the time the manager looked back there was no-one there.

Keep a look out for the gentleman dressed in tweed who stands by the bar. He has been seen by both staff and customers but always disappears by the time staff go to serve him. The pub also has a poltergeist, nicknamed Henry, who lies quiet for long periods of time and then gets back to his old tricks. A favourite is to hide the ice cream scoops. They can disappear for weeks at a time and then suddenly turn up in a really obvious place.

The cellar is often subject to odd smells such as heavy sweat, pipe tobacco and oddly expensive perfume. One of these smells has quite a sad story behind it. Many years ago, an infant died in the pub and the body was laid out in the cellar before the funeral. Apparently, the infant's mother always liked to wear expensive perfume.

The White Hart
High Street
Shifnal
TF11 8BH

52.670898, -2.372190

The White Hart dates back to 1620 and was a coaching inn serving mainly the horsemen who would work the frequent London stagecoaches. It is hardly surprising that a building with such a long history can lay claim to a ghost or two.

In the upstairs living accommodation, a little girl with blond hair has been seen entering one of the bedrooms. She appears to be a perfectly real little girl except that when the bedroom is checked of course there is no-one there. Who she is or why she haunts the pub is a complete mystery.

Nearby Weston Park often hosts re-enactment events, so it is not unusual to sometimes see people in period costume. On one occasion after just such an event a costumed character was seen in the main bar waiting to be served. The Landlord had a very clear view of the man. He was dressed in a blue tunic with a red kerchief around his neck. On his head, he had a pointed hat with a wide brim. He was sporting a full beard and a brown belt was fastened across his chest. As if waiting to be served he was holding out some sort of pewter jug. The Landlord only glanced away for a moment but in that instant the oddly dressed man was gone. The bar was completely empty.

This wasn't quite the end of the story as the Landlord's dog started behaving strangely in the bar. His hair standing on end and growling as if someone was still in there.

White Ladies Priory
Shackerley Lane
Codsall Wood
WV8 1QY

52.665774, -2.258537

About a mile from Boscobel House on the same lane towards Cosford lies White Ladies Priory. Once a medieval Augustinian Nunnery, all that remains now is a ruin which can be accessed on foot down a narrow track. It was the Priory of St Leonard dating back to at least 1186. White Ladies got its name from the nuns, canonesses who wore white robes.

Charles II sheltered here for a short while after escaping the Battle of Worcester. By this time, what little was left of White Ladies Priory after the dissolution of the monasteries had been converted into a house.

White Ladies is an eerie place even on a nice sunny day. Many people feel very uneasy here and that someone or something is constantly watching them. The Priory is approached on foot along a narrow track and here too the sense of being watched can be quite intense.

A number of strange things have been reported here. White clad figures have been seen drifting through the ruins as have odd balls of light. The faint but unmistakable sounds of religious chanting are heard but the source can never be traced. Odd mists appear and vanish just as quickly but often turn up on photographs taken at White Ladies Priory.

Smethwick

Black Patch Park
Access from Woodburn Road
Smethwick
B66 2PU

52.499183, -1.944567

The oddly named Black Patch was home to a community of gypsies during the 19th and very early 20th centuries. It most likely got its name from the black furnace waste dumped there from Mathew Boulton's foundries. More recently, evidence has come to light that Charlie Chaplin came from a gypsy family and was born in a caravan on Black Patch.

Esau and his wife Sentinia (Henty) Smith were undisputed King and Queen of the gypsies. Esau died in 1901 and was survived by Queen Henty, as she was known, until she also passed away in 1907. Queen Henty died believing that they had a legal right to Black Patch. Despite this there were evictions in 1905 and 1909 and plans to develop the land. It is said that the document to prove ownership was destroyed when Queen Henty's caravan was destroyed by fire in very suspicious circumstances. In order to try and protect this right, Queen Henty is said to have placed a curse on anyone who tried to build on the land. The initial plans to build a housing estate on the site eventually came to nothing when Black Patch was made a park in 1909.

Is it the ghost of Queen Henty who still haunts Black Patch Park? Certainly, stories of a woman dressed in black suddenly appearing in the park have persisted for many years. She is generally described as an old woman wearing a black dress with a bright red cape and jet-black hair. Plans to develop Black Patch Park again were successfully fought off by a local friend's group in 2007. Queen Henty would certainly have approved.

Harry Mitchell Leisure Centre
Broomfield
Smethwick
B67 7DH

52.491129, -1.975432

The Harry Mitchell Centre started life as a drill hall donated by Henry Mitchell of the Mitchells and Butlers brewery. He presented it to Smethwick Corporation and the Staffordshire Volunteer Reserves in 1898 in memory of his son, Henry Mitchell Junior, known as 'Harry' to family and friends. Harry, a keen sportsman, died a premature death in 1894 when he contracted Typhoid Fever aged just 32.

During the Second World War, the Territorial Army Paymaster was required to stay overnight in the drill hall on occasions. He was generally accompanied by his son. Around 1.00am in the morning they would regularly hear loud footsteps as if someone was walking purposefully through the building. The Paymaster was so troubled by these regular disturbances that he was quite ready to fire his army pistol had any figure actually appeared. But of course, none ever did.

The Paymaster and his son were both convinced that it was the ghost of Harry Mitchell patrolling the building donated in his memory. Even after the war, when the drill hall became the leisure centre it is today, the footsteps continued. And they still do. Echoing around the old drill hall in the early hours of the morning.

Smethwick Swimming Centre
Thimblemill Road
Smethwick
B67 5QT

52.480168, -1.974823

Smethwick Swimming Centre is a Grade II listed Art Deco building which opened in 1933. During World War II the building served as a community air raid shelter. It was also used as a civil defence base and when necessary, a morgue. An American supply base was housed nearby together with a group of Italian prisoners of war.

The baths have been subject to almost constant paranormal activity going right back to the 1930s. The ghosts of three children, two boys and a girl, have been seen regularly or heard laughing and playing when the building should be empty. They are often heard when staff are locking up at night.

Extensive service corridors run under the pool area and this is where much of the wartime activity took place. It is here that a man dressed in a green boiler suit is seen. He seems to know when machinery is about to break down and is more likely to be seen by people who are new to the tunnels. He seems to be a maintenance man who can't bear to leave his old place of work.

In the old air raid shelter an American in full dress uniform has been seen together with a character described as a war time spiv and an Italian prisoner of war. An airman in German uniform has also been seen who may be associated with a Luftwaffe plane shot down in the area. It is believed the pilot was brought into the tunnels for interrogation by the Americans.

In February 2009, the author was involved in an extensive investigation of the tunnels beneath the swimming baths. At 12.15am a male figure was briefly seen by the old air raid shelter. Perhaps he thought there was some problem with the pool machinery as he was the ghost in the green boiler suit.

Thimblemill Library
Thimblemill Road
Smethwick
B67 5RJ

52.481538, -1.976566

Thimblemill Library is an attractive, Art Deco Moderne style building dating back to 1937. Since 2003, it has held Grade II listed building status. The name comes from a former corn mill which was situated nearby and remained at least until the late 1880s. The corn-mill was converted to the manufacture of thimbles, hence the rather unusual name. Thimblemill Library hosts regular and varied activities for the local community including, appropriately enough, Halloween events.

Over a period of many years both staff and library users have experienced unusual activity here. According to staff the library is haunted by an old lady in a long dress who has been seen particularly in the main library area. She is described as looking like an old-style school mistress, although seems much more likely to be a prim and proper librarian from the days when libraries were much more formal establishments than they are now. In any event, she certainly appears stern enough to make today's staff feel very uneasy when they are working there on their own in the building.

On a paranormal investigation here a few years back, although nothing was witnessed personally by the author, the library area certainly took on an eerie feeling at times during the night. Almost as though we were being closely watched.

Warley Woods
Lightwoods Hill
Smethwick
B67 5ED

52.469123, -1.982156

Warley Woods was once the Warley Hall Estate, created after the dissolution of the monasteries by Henry VIII. Samuel Galton II purchased the estate in 1792 and commissioned Humphrey Repton to landscape the grounds and Robert Lugar to build Warley Abbey in the then popular gothic style. By the 1950s this house had fell into disrepair and was sadly demolished in 1957.

Documented reports of a 'grey lady' haunting Warley woods go back as far as 1822. There are many theories as to who she might be including one that she is the grief-stricken widow of a military man who hung herself from one of the trees in the woods. Whoever she is, the phantom lady is described as wearing a long grey dress and carrying an air of authority as she sweeps by.

Other apparitions reported here include a soldier in an old fashioned red uniform who wanders the area where Abbey House once stood. Whether or not he is associated with the 'grey lady' is of course open to speculation.

Another enduring story from the area concerns the 'Chinese man'. He is reputed to have been the servant of an old lady who lived in a gamekeeper's cottage on the estate. His ghost continues to be seen around the area where he was employed in life. This story may have connections with a Chinese labourer, Zee Ming Wu, who was robbed and murdered in the park in 1919.

In 1822 Sam Whitehouse was robbed and murdered in the woods. Joseph Downing was accused of his murder but escaped the gallows after the defence that Sam had been thrown from his horse when it was startled by the ghost of the 'grey lady' was accepted by the court! Sam obviously disapproved of the verdict as his angry ghost still wanders the woods to this day.

Stourbridge

Badger's Sett
Hagley
Stourbridge
DY9 9JS

52.431161, -2.105051

Originally, the Badger's Sett was called The Gypsy's Tent. The present building dates back to 1938, but the previous pub on the same site was late Victorian. It was renamed the Badger's Sett in 1983. Both the present pub and the A456 Hagley Road it sits on (see page 100) are subject to paranormal activity.

The Gypsy's Tent is very much associated with the local story of Bella in the Wych Elm. In 1943 four schoolboys discovered the skeleton of a woman hidden in a tree in nearby Hagley Wood. She had one hand missing and her mouth was stuffed with taffeta and a gold wedding ring. The pathologist's report at the time determined that she was about 35 years of age and had died, probably of asphyxiation, around 1941. Various theories about who she was and why she was murdered have been put forward. Was she the victim of witchcraft, a jealous lover or had she uncovered an alleged German wartime spy ring in the area?

Nobody knows for certain but staff at the Badger's Sett maintain that Bella makes her presence felt by turning lights on and off after hours, opening and closing doors and moving things around. If it is Bella, then she is not alone as the ghost of a gentleman in a tweed jacket has been reported in and around the pub. Unlike Bella he has been seen briefly on occasions by both staff and customers. He likes to lean against the bar before vanishing.

Hagley Road Ghosts
Pedmore
Stourbridge
DY9 9JS

52.431000, -2.103833

Just where the A456 Hagley Road passes the Badger's Sett pub between Halesowen and Hagley is one of the most haunted stretches of road in the country. And the paranormal activity is not just restricted to the road as the Badger's Sett pub is also haunted (see page 99).

Over the years a plethora of sightings have been made along here including that of a little girl who wanders down the dual carriageway before disappearing. Bodies in the road have also been reported together with shadowy figures lurking at the side of the road. Some sightings are even more unnerving and frighten drivers into thinking they have run somebody over.

Typical of these reports was the experience of a now retired police officer when returning home after work at about 1.00am one morning. He saw a figure running across the carriageway from the direction of the Badger's Sett. His initial thought was that the man was coming from a fancy-dress party as he was in full cavalier style attire, big hat, knee length boots and a red uniform complete with sword. The figure stopped on the central reservation but as the officer approached launched himself directly in front of the car.

Despite slamming the brakes on hard enough to spin the car the policeman was convinced he had killed someone. Shaking from the experience, he got out and started looking for the body. There was no body, and indeed no sign of the strangely dressed figure at all. Not only that, there was no damage to the car and thinking about it later the officer realised there had been no sound of a collision apart from the screech of his own brakes.

Bonded Warehouse
2 Canal Street
Stourbridge
DY8 4LU

52.460963, -2.149561

The Bonded Warehouse is a three storey canal side building with some parts dating back to 1799. Originally the building was used to securely store taxable goods such as tobacco, spirits and tea brought by canal until the appropriate excise duties had been paid. Nowadays the building plays host to many events including paranormal investigations and is often open to the public.

A variety of strange activities are reported here by both staff and visitors. Objects get moved around, doors open and close by themselves and figures are seen.

On the top floor, a series of visible heavy roof trusses create a large open space beneath. This area is said to be haunted by a little girl who skips and plays together with an old boatman seen up in the rafters. Not quite as bizarre as it sounds as the roof space above the rafters was probably once boarded over and used for storage. This gentleman has also been glimpsed standing silently in the middle of the floor.

The playful little girl may have made her presence felt during a recent paranormal investigation attended by the author. A trigger object, in this case a child's ball, had been positioned on the top floor. Having been there for some time the ball was filmed suddenly bouncing across the room. There was no-one anywhere near the trigger object at the time.

Mary Stevens Park
Worcester Street
Stourbridge
DY8 2DA

52.450528, -2.150742

Mary Stevens Park was created by Ernest Stevens in memory of his wife. Mary Stevens had died prematurely in 1925. The public park opened in 1931 on land which had once been the Studley Court Estate. Ernest also financed the magnificent front gates of Portland stone and wrought iron.

These gates lead out directly onto the Worcester Street island. It is here, rather than Mary Stevens Park itself, that a rather strange ghost was seen by very credible witnesses.

Two policemen in a Panda car on a late-night shift were confronted by a bizarre sight. Coming from the direction of the gates they spotted an old man going around the island and heading off towards Heath Street. Nothing too strange about that but instead of walking the old gentleman was floating along the road.

They followed him into Heath Street and watched him float down the left-hand side of the road. His legs were obscured by parked cars, but the figure was unmistakably floating along rather than walking. He got to about half way along the street and then he simply vanished to the amazement of the officers. Despite a thorough search of the area no trace of the strange floating gentleman could be found. The whole street was quiet and deserted, as it should be in the early hours of the morning.

Somerset House
Enville Street
Stourbridge
DY8 3TQ

52.458213, -2.154859

The former Somerset House pub dates right back to 1835. It ceased to be a public house in 2013 and has since been used for offices. The Somerset House had a long history of ghostly goings on. This is possibly associated with bodies being temporarily stored in the cellar in the 1940s whilst coffins were being assembled at the rear of the premises. But this wasn't the reason the public house was to hit the national headlines in the late 1990s.

In 1998 a most unusual phenomenon was noticed on the premises which generated a great deal of interest at the time. Full pints of beer pressed against the wallpaper would remain suspended there as if held up by some invisible hand. There was no doubt that the phenomenon was real as it was well documented and photographed. What caused intense speculation at the time was why this was happening. Given that the pub already claimed to be haunted it is no surprise that one theory suggested that a ghost was holding the glasses there!

Along with local paranormal teams, experts from Wolverhampton University were called in to try and get to the bottom of the mystery. The general consensus of opinion was that the old wallpaper had absorbed cigarette smoke over the years and that this had reacted with the ink to form an adhesive. A very logical explanation, or was something more paranormal involved given the history of the building?

Starving Rascal
Brettell Lane
Stourbridge
DY8 4BN

52.472599, -2.144655

The Starving Rascal is a mid-Victorian public house which was originally called The Dudley Arms. It was only renamed the Starving Rascal in 1974 in recognition of a tragic event which took place in Victorian times.

A beggar turned up at the pub door during a particularly harsh winter to ask for some food, drink and a little comfort. He found none of this at the Dudley Arms. The landlord cruelly turned him away into the freezing cold. Before dying of exposure and malnutrition on the steps outside the beggar placed a curse on the pub.

It is this beggar who is said to haunt the pub. Wet footprints can appear on the floor even when the weather is dry, and staff and customers alike have both felt and seen a figure described as an old man in various parts of the pub. He has been seen sitting at the bar and entering the gentlemen's toilet.

Beer glasses have been known to start swinging on their hooks as if someone was pushing them. This is also a pub to watch out for your own beer glass. Customers have had the experience of seeing a hand reach out to grab their pint from them only to find there is nobody there.

The author has been involved in paranormal investigations here in the past and whilst nothing conclusive was found, nevertheless an elusive shadow was seen more than once flitting around the bar in the early hours.

Stourbridge Police Club
New Road (Stourbridge Police Station)
Stourbridge
DY8 1PF

52.455034, -2.145385

Once an Inspector's house the building now houses Stourbridge Police Club. It has been subject to a large number of strange occurrences earning a reputation for being haunted. The club stands in the grounds of Stourbridge Police Station which is itself haunted (see page 106).

In the early hours of one morning a police officer on night duty went into the bar on his break to eat his sandwiches. The building was deserted but a man suddenly appeared at the bar dressed in normal street clothes. He was looking towards the pool room as if waiting for someone to come out. Before the astonished officer could do or say anything the man vanished away into thin air.

The ladies' toilet is situated at the end of a long corridor. On many occasions ladies using the toilets report clearly hearing loud footsteps coming along the corridor and stopping immediately outside the toilet door. Assuming someone is waiting to use the toilet, they are amazed to find no one there when they open the cubicle door.

Family events are sometimes run at the club and children playing in the hallway have found themselves talking to a little girl around seven or eight years of age. No one knows who this little girl is, but she certainly doesn't come in with any of the present-day customers.

Stourbridge Police Station
New Road
Stourbridge
DY8 1PF

52.454692, -2.145033

Stourbridge Police Station opened in 1911 and the imposing building also incorporated a new Magistrate's Court. Previously, prisoners had to be marched through Stourbridge to the County Court in Hagley Road. The more genteel of Stourbridge folk were naturally not impressed with this arrangement. The new building allowed prisoners to be transferred internally between the cells and the court above.

With such a long history it is no great surprise that the building is haunted. And not just the police station itself. The old Inspector's house in the grounds, which now houses the Police Club, is also haunted (see page 105).

The cells under Stourbridge Police Station are in a long passageway with an alcove halfway down with sinks for washing. A set of stairs leads up to the old court. On one occasion, the duty custody officer was taking a prisoner back to one of the cells. He noticed a man in non-descript civilian looking clothes leaning over one of the sinks having a wash. Knowing there should not have been anyone else down there, and after locking up his prisoner, the officer looked back towards the alcove to see who it was. The passageway and alcove were both empty and there was nowhere the man could possibly have gone.

The Talbot Hotel
High Street
Stourbridge
DY8 1DW

52.457082, -2.146638

The Talbot Hotel dates back to the 1630s and for much of its life was a coaching inn. However, it was originally the home of Richard Foley (1580 – 1667) who was a rich and influential local ironmaster. As a later coaching inn, the Talbot played host to a number of prominent organisations and was both a social and business centre in Stourbridge. The Talbot retains many original features but like most buildings has been developed over time.

Not surprisingly for such an old building there is an extensive network of cellars beneath the building which extend under the street and the adjacent shops. These tunnels are closely connected with the paranormal activity here and take on a frightening and oppressive atmosphere at times.

A particularly sad story is behind the reported haunting at the Talbot Hotel. In the 18th Century a landlord had an illicit affair with a young lady, most likely a servant girl, who fell pregnant by him. The baby was stillborn, and he hid the body behind one of the walls of the cellar in order to hide evidence of the affair. Shortly afterwards the mother also died, most likely from complications following the difficult birth. Room 19 was reputed to be their bed chamber and where the unfortunate girl probably lost her own life.

Since then the Talbot Hotel has been haunted by the apparition of a lady in white who wanders all over the building but particularly in the area around Room 19. She has been seen by staff and residents alike. A forlorn figure, sobbing and searching in vain for her lost baby.

Tettenhall

Beacon Radio Studios
267 Tettenhall Road
Tettenhall
WV6 0DE

52.594912, -2.156881

The former Beacon Radio studios in Tettenhall Road was housed in the large 19th century Normanhurst House. After purchasing the property in the mid-1970s, Beacon Radio 303, as it was known then, first went on the air in 1976. Throughout the radio station's time in Tettenhall there were regular reports from the staff there that the building was haunted.

There is speculation that Normanhurst House was once a children's home or orphanage at some time during the late Victorian and early Edwardian period. Whilst there is no tangible evidence available for this nevertheless staff who worked at the studios were convinced that the building was haunted by the ghosts of Victorian children.

The children have been heard playing and singing in the upstairs part of the house. Also, the haunting sound of a little baby crying coming from one of the rooms. Unexplained temperature drops have been felt throughout the building, together with feelings of not being alone and shadowy figures seen.

Children have been sighted here at times and the main staircase is a particular hotspot. As well as the children in Victorian clothes, a rather stern lady has been seen here and even more alarming some staff claimed to have been pushed on the stairs. Was she the matron of the old orphanage perhaps?

Tettenhall Towers
Wood Road
Tettenhall
WV6 8QX

52.595410, -2.169670

Tettenhall Towers was the former home of the extremely eccentric and flamboyant Colonel Thomas Thorneycroft. He got his rank from being a Lieutenant Colonel in the Staffordshire Yeomanry. Tettenhall Towers is now in the grounds of Tettenhall College. Colonel Thorneycroft purchased the building in 1853 and built the distinctive water tower in 1866. He was something of an inventor and thought nothing of launching terrified servants off the roof of his tower to test his ideas for flying machines. There is no record of whether or not they survived!

The building today retains the original theatre built by the Colonel and is a strange place. Indeed, Colonel Thorneycroft himself is said to still wander his former home and dark, shadowy figures are to be seen flitting around the many rooms in this most mysterious of places.

Small rooms upstairs known as the Doll's House are subject to paranormal activity. Footsteps are heard when there is no one there, children's voices have been heard and objects thrown around.

On a paranormal investigation here, the author and a colleague were sitting in an area of the Doll's House which is quite difficult to enter through a tight entrance. Whilst in there we clearly heard footsteps come up the stairs and enter the room outside our area. Fully expecting someone to make themselves known we called out to them. No answer, and what is more the room was empty. Everyone in our group was accounted for and no-one had been in the Doll's House apart from us.

Tipton

Fountain Inn
Owen Street
Tipton
DY4 8HE

52.528716, -2.069932

The Fountain Inn in Tipton dates back to at least 1828 and is well known locally for being associated with the legendary boxer, William Perry, known as the 'Tipton Slasher'. He is reputed to have used the attic of the pub for training. This may explain the ghostly figure of a sporting gentleman who has been seen here.

William Perry came from a boating family and had learnt his trade fighting tough canal boatmen for prime position when passing through busy lock gates. He went on to become the bare knuckle heavyweight champion of England between 1850 and 1857.

Often ghosts are only witnessed by one person at a time but not here. The Fountain boasts a rare group sighting of an apparition some years back seen upstairs in the attic area.

Some years ago, the landlord and landlady were showing a small group of guests where the Tipton Slasher used to train. As they opened the door all present witnessed the apparition of a man sitting on a chair in the middle of the room. The man was in shorts and had black, centre parted hair and a large moustache. To their amazement the figure simply disappeared.

Unfortunately, the sighting does not in any way match the nearby statue of William Perry so perhaps this apparition is another boxer or sparring partner rather than the legendary Tipton Slasher himself.

The Park Inn
Victoria Road
Tipton
DY4 8SS

52.523866, -2.057457

The former Park Inn closed in 1996 and was converted into flats. As far as is known the building is no longer subject to any paranormal activity. Originally built as a hotel, the Park dates to around 1900. It was reputed to be haunted by the ghost of a little girl, Lady May. A rather grand title perhaps but she was the young daughter of a Leicestershire Squire who often visited the area on business. He would sometimes bring his daughter with him and she had her own room up in the attic.

On one of these visits Lady May suffered a bad nosebleed after going out riding with her father. She was instructed to go to her room and lie down while her father attended to his business. By the time he returned it was too late for poor little Lady May. She was already dead. Piecing together what had happened it seems that Lady May's nosebleed had got very much worse. She had tried to get out of the attic to summon help, but the door had jammed trapping her inside.

After this the attic took on a more frightening atmosphere. Footsteps and bangs would be heard coming from the empty room. Dogs would often refuse to go anywhere near. The lights would come on by themselves. On one occasion, the wife of a former landlord was in the attic on her own which always made her feel uneasy. She felt something push past her towards the attic door which then slowly closed and latched behind her. Just as though someone had just left.

The Pie Factory
Hurst Lane
Tipton
DY4 9AB

52.529616, -2.076741

The present building was opened in 1923 as the Doughty Arms. It was named after Councillor William Woolley Doughty JP, who was chairman of the local licensing magistrates at the time. This replaced an earlier mid-Victorian pub called the Five Ways. It became the Pie Factory in 1987.

Three ghosts are said to haunt the Pie Factory. One apparition is never seen clearly but has been described as possibly being a Cavalier from the English Civil War. There was a battle at Tipton Green in 1644 which is not too far away and nearby Dudley Castle was a Royalist stronghold. However, it must be noted that even the older Five Ways pub was built far too late to have any direct Civil War connections.

The pub is also haunted by what seems to be a little girl. Associated mainly with the cellar, she can sometimes be heard singing down there. Although as yet she has never been seen, she has certainly been heard running up the cellar steps and laughing.

The most active is an apparition known as Nobby. He is said to be a former landlord who chose to hang himself in the cellar. Nobby is seen wearing a long black cloak but is by no means restricted to the cellar, being seen occasionally in other parts of the pub. He also has the unfortunate habit of pulling at men's clothing whilst they are standing in the gentleman's toilet!

The Noahs Ark
Wood Street
Tipton
DY4 9BQ

52.530327, -2.068250

The Noah's Ark originally had a beerhouse licence with the earliest record of the pub going back to 1841. However, the haunting here is associated with a much later time. Between 1933 and 1944 the landlord was Thomas (Tom) Cartwright, an ex-professional boxer. He continued to manage boxers and train them in a gym behind the pub. Tom Cartwright was a man who stood no nonsense from anyone.

One night, Tom was rudely awoken by a figure he took to be an intruder. Naturally he brought his boxing skills to bear and attempted to floor the man standing by his bed. As his fists were passing straight through the young man, he suddenly vanished into thin air.

This was not to be only sighting of the ghostly young man. His next visitation was to Tom's wife Mildred (Milda) who recalled some details of what he was wearing. He was a young man in a tweed suit with fair hair and brown eyes. She described him as looking perfectly solid and not at all frightening as he looked so serene. In fact, she only realised he was an apparition at all when the young man disappeared in front of her.

This wasn't the end of the story though as older customers in the pub were able to identify the ghostly figure from Milda's description. He was the nineteen-year-old son of a previous landlord who had met an untimely death.

Trysull

Bridgnorth Road
Tinker's Cross
Trysull
WV5 7AX

52.541285, -2.263981

The Bridgnorth Road beyond Wombourne has stories of phantom hitchhikers and strange figures seen at the side of the road. One such story concerns a coach driver who had dropped off a party of pensioners in Bridgnorth one Sunday evening in October 2000 and was heading back to the coach station in Gornal.

On the way back, he had just passed The Wheel at Worfield when he saw a man carrying a petrol can at the side of the road. Clearly the man had run out of petrol and so the driver, Stuart, stopped to pick him up. The man gratefully boarded the coach and sat in the courier's seat. He explained that his car, a rare Triumph TR8, had run out of petrol.

Stuart recalls that the man had a slightly out of date 1970s hair style and clothes to match. He said his car was at Tinker's Cross just outside of Trysull. It was on Stuart's way back, and so he offered to drop the man off by his car. Sure enough, the car was pulled up on the verge. Stuart remembers saying, "there's your TR7" and the man corrected him by saying it was a rarer TR8.

On pulling up the coach the man thanked Stuart and got out on the near side. He walked right in front of the coach windscreen and across to his car. Stuart prepared to pull off and looked out of the driver's window to check the road was clear. It certainly was. No broken-down car and no sign of the strange hitchhiker. Tinker's Cross was deserted.

Plough Inn
School Road
Trysull
WV5 7HR

52.543656, -2.220454

The Grade II listed Plough Inn is thought to have originally been a farmhouse which became a pub following Wellington's 1830 Beer Act. It later became an inn offering basic accommodation and food in addition to home brewed ales.

Although the Plough has been an inn since 1833 the building itself is much older and dates back to at least the sixteenth century. One of the upstairs rooms contains a rare surviving example of Tudor wall paintings which were quite common before the reformation. This room is known locally as 'The Devil's Room'. For whilst the paintings mainly depict birds and a horse being led there is also an image of what appears to be the Devil leading an animal or child with a smaller impish figure dancing nearby.

A number of apparitions have been experienced here over the years. A previous landlady reported seeing a monk in a brown habit. She described the figure as seeming to be quite solid and real but not of this time. A figure has also been seen passing quickly through the pub and one previous landlord had a most unnerving experience when a tall lady tried to drag him into the kitchen before promptly disappearing.

More recently, and at different times, staff have seen a gentleman standing at the end of the bar. When they go to serve him, there is no one there. Even more intriguingly there is nowhere the mysterious man could have gone.

Village Green
School Road
Trysull
WV5 7HW

52.542153, -2.221582

The ancient village green at Trysull used to be known as Bent Green. It lies a little further along School Road from the Plough Inn which is also haunted (see page 115). Traditionally, the village green would have been used for communal activities such as May Day celebrations.

The village green is reputed to be haunted by a whole group of children, interestingly very similar to those seen behind the Crooked House in Himley (see page 60) but equally inexplicable.

Caroline, one of the barmaids who worked at the Red Lion Wombourne in the 1980s, would often witness an eerie re-enactment on her way home from work. She would be driving home alone, and her route took her along School Road and past the old village green.

By the time the pub had closed it would often be around midnight when Caroline would be passing the village green. She described regularly seeing a group of young looking children on the green dancing round in a circle. Were they dancing around an unseen maypole perhaps?

Strange enough to see such young children out so late at night but these children were certainly not of our time. Not judging by the old fashioned clothes they were wearing anyway.

Wall Heath

Mile Flat
Wall Heath
DY6 0AL

52.503475, -2.191693

Swindon Road near the Mile Flat crossroads has been subject to a number of reports involving phantom accidents. Intriguingly, the reports are broadly similar but differ in the detail of who, and what, was involved. They all concern the same stretch of road and take place near to where the old Waggon and Horses pub used to stand on the crossroads.

A motorist driving in the direction of Kingswinford one night witnessed a collision between a car and a bicycle on the opposite side of the road. He brought his car to a halt just beyond where the accident had occurred. On getting out to see if anyone had been hurt he realised that the road was deserted, with no sign of an accident ever having taken place.

Near midnight some years ago two young friends and their girlfriends were in a car driving back home towards Kingswinford. When they were passing the rugby club they drove into an unexpected heavy mist. A figure in a grey coat suddenly ran from the right-hand side of the road right in front of their car. The occupants were convinced they had hit him as he seemed to be thrown off the bonnet. In a state of shock, the driver screeched the car to a halt and they all got out to see if they could help the man they were convinced they had hit. By the time they got out of the car the strange mist had vanished. There was no sign of a body, no damage to the car and nowhere the man could possibly have gone.

Walsall

Bentley Hall
Cairn Drive
Bentley
WS2 0HW

52.589000, -2.020833

Bentley Hall was sadly demolished in 1929. The surrounding area had been undermined for coal and there was a danger that this once grand hall would collapse. Its location was commemorated by a cairn erected by Walsall Historical Association in 1934.

During the English Civil War Bentley Hall was one of the places that hid Charles II after his defeat by the Parliamentarians at the battle of Worcester in 1651. He was sheltered by Colonel John Lane who owned the hall at the time. It was his sister, Jane Lane, who was to ensure that Charles safely escaped to Bristol disguised as her servant.

No real wonder then that the site is allegedly haunted by an English Civil War soldier. He has been seen in full Cavalier dress and has been described as being quite a jovial sort of character. He appears to have a particular penchant for the ladies. The ghost is known locally as Charlie, but this probably has more to do with the Charles II connection than anything else.

Charlie seems to have been particularly active in the 1960s with a number of sightings including the Reverend Raymond Wilcox of the nearby Emmanuel Church. Controversially, Wilcox eventually confessed to having made up the stories of Charlie. However, no-one appears to have told Charlie himself as he continued his ghostly activities unabated!

Manor Arms
Park Road
Rushall
WS4 1LG

52.601500, -1.954000

The Manor Arms is Grade II listed and was originally a farmhouse. Indeed, the Anson family who owned it continued to farm the area after obtaining a beerhouse license in the early 1860s for the purposes of selling beer to passing boatmen. This was converted to a full public house licence around 1895.

The canal runs immediately behind the pub and the bargees were a good source of trade. The building is mainly 18th century but parts of it are believed to date back to the 15th and 16th centuries. It is known locally as 'the pub with no bar' as the beer pulls are set in the wall. A central corridor divides the building and it is here that one of the several ghosts is seen.

A tall, dark male figure walks along this ground floor passage at times much to the amazement of pub regulars who like to congregate here to enjoy their drinks. Another well-known apparition here is that of a former landlady. She is said to have died in the pub after falling down some steps, possibly in the cellar. Her ghost is seen wearing a white dress and a summery straw hat. Two phantom children are also linked with the building although there are no details as to who they might be or why they are in the pub.

Local legend has it that monks inhabited the area in the 12th century and indeed the ghost of a monk has reputedly been seen in the pub. Unfortunately, there is no historical record of monks, thirsty or otherwise, ever having resided here.

St Matthew's Church
St Matthew's Close
Walsall
WS1 3DG

52.582450, -1.977426

St Matthew's Church looks out over the busy town of Walsall as it has done for hundreds of years. Alterations to the church were made in the 15th and 19th centuries but the inner crypt is reputed to be the oldest surviving man-made construction in Walsall and dates all the way back to the 13th century.

The church has some interesting legends and stories associated with it. The first is that the original location for the church was not approved of by the local faerie folk and so they moved the foundation stones to the top of the hill where the church stands now. An enduring, although unlikely, story is that tunnels intersect in the crypt of the church and one leads off to the White Hart at Claldmore Green which itself is haunted (see page 126).

Another story has it that during the reformation of the monasteries escaping monks were walled up alive in one of the tunnels. There has been no sign of ghostly monks as far as is known but there are reports of a medieval lady dressed in a long blue dress who glides silently across the stone floor in the earliest part of the crypt before vanishing.

Market Tavern
High Street
Walsall
WS1 1QR

52.583192, -1.979629

The former Market Tavern is closed at present. It has been a pub since mid-Victorian times and the building occupies a prominent position alongside a street market which can trace its origins back to medieval times. When the pub was being refurbished by the Highgate Brewery a few years ago an ancient set of stocks was discovered in the cellar. No doubt many a local miscreant suffered the ignominy of being locked up in public.

During this refurbishment the workmen involved were continuously plagued by tools being moved and going missing. The cellar bar area particularly had an uncomfortable atmosphere and one unfortunate workman was to find out why.

On his way out one evening the workman was confronted by the sight of a disembodied head. The head was hooded like a monk and floating a few feet above the ground. After looking away in terror the apparition thankfully disappeared. Even so, the workman refused to ever go down into the cellar alone again.

Even after the refurbishment was completed, shadowy figures were seen in the cellar and on one occasion the sound of a heavy bench being moved was heard although nothing was seen. A past resident of the building, an old lady, has been seen wandering around the first floor and the kitchen area. On one occasion one of the chefs saw her reflection in a mirror. She passed straight through a solid wall where years before there was once a doorway.

Shelfield Ghost Train
Lichfield Road
Shelfield
WS4 1PU

52.617098, -1.951254

The Leighswood branch line which ran through Shelfield in Walsall was opened in 1878 but closed to trains in the mid-1960s. This single-track freight only railway line mainly serviced a number of brickworks and also the Leighswood Colliery.

The deep cutting leading to Four Crosses Road running under the Lichfield Road has long since been filled in leaving just the upper section of the west wall of the bridge remaining. Nevertheless, the unmistakeable sounds and smells of a steam engine on the single-track line beneath the long gone bridge have been experienced by passers-by on the Lichfield Road.

A local story provides a possible explanation as to why there should be a steam engine experienced in this particular spot. A little further up the road is a Co-op supermarket which used to be the Spring Cottage Public House.

The story goes that back when the line was in regular use the driver and fireman of a shunter nearing the end of their night shift would often leave the engine steaming beneath the bridge. They would walk the short distance up the road to the Spring Cottage in order to enjoy a few pints of beer before taking the shunter back to the engine sheds. It seems old habits die hard.

The Black Country Arms
High Street
Walsall
WS1 1QW

52.583298, -1.979262

The Black Country Arms was formerly The Green Dragon and is recorded as far back as 1627 when it was part of the municipal buildings. It became part of the Magistrate's Court in 1910 but is now returned to its former use as a pub.

There are a number of stories associated with the pub including people feeling someone is standing right behind them on the stairs and sightings of a ghostly hound in the building. However, the most frequently reported ghost haunting the pub is a lady in a blue dress who stands in a second-floor window. Because a floor was taken out to create a higher ceiling it is no longer possible for someone to be standing in that particular window.

The son of one of the landlords of the Green Dragon managed to produce a very detailed drawing of the Blue Lady and the dress she was wearing. Claire Dolman, who was working for Walsall Museum at the time, conducted some very interesting research into the likely time period of the lady's attire.

As a result of this research a good possibility is that she is Mary Hemming. Mary had married Deykin Hemming in 1755 and they lived together in the building during the 1700s. Despite losing three of her six young children Mary appears to have been happy here. Perhaps this is why she has apparently never left.

The Starting Gate
16 Newport Street
Walsall
WS1 1RZ

52.582643, -1.982993

The unusually named Starting Gate used to be called the Stand Tavern. This is a reference back to a time when Walsall had a racecourse alongside what is now Bradford Street. Horse racing took place here from 1754 to 1876. The Starting Gate was up for sale at the time of writing.

A good deal of activity has been reported at the Starting Gate including many newspaper reports of the alleged paranormal happenings here. The ghost haunting the pub is nicknamed 'Ethel' and is reputed to be a previous landlady. Ethel May Freeman was landlady here for many years between 1945 and 1960. Her white, shimmering figure has been seen flitting across the cellar on a number of occasions. Ethel is generally accompanied by a strong smell of perfume. In common with other reports of hauntings the paranormal activity here is often accompanied by an intense cold.

Loud footsteps have also been heard on the upper floor of the building when there has been no one upstairs at the time. People commonly hear their name being called even though there is no-one there. Poltergeist type activity has also been reported here including a glass flying off a shelf in the bar in full view of a previous landlord. Curiously on a couple of occasions untidy bedrooms have been mysteriously tidied up. On another occasion, the door to the bedroom was found to be blocked by a quilt and a pile of sheets from off the bed. The bed had only just been made.

The Wheatsheaf
4 Birmingham Road
Walsall
WS1 2NA

52.580653, -1.975620

The Wheatsheaf is a very old hostelry and was certainly recorded as trading as early as 1801. It was originally known as The Greyhound and kept this name up until around the 1820s when it was changed to The Wheatsheaf.

This is a very active building as far as the supernatural is concerned. Frequently after the pub is closed for the night the doors start banging and loud footsteps are often heard in the bar area. When the pub is open, customer's drinks often get moved around although no-one ever actually sees the glasses move. The poltergeist type activity here even goes as far as breaking certain objects. On one occasion a number of glass framed pictures were found to be lying shattered on a bedroom floor. No-one had heard anything and in any case, the bedroom floor was heavily carpeted. Also in one of the bedrooms a carefully folded skirt went missing. It was quickly found downstairs. Draped over one of the tills in the bar.

Electrical equipment often gets interfered with. At one time the lights would regularly turn on and off and the alarm would go off in the early hours for no reason. Wet footprints were also seen by the cleaner in the just cleaned bar. Whilst no-one was seen on this occasion an apparition has been seen striding purposefully through the bar. He was dressed in what one of the regulars described as an RAF uniform but from World War Two.

The White Hart
Caldmore Green
Walsall
WS1 3RW

52.576602, -1.983174

Now preserved and converted to residential flats the former White Hart Inn dates back to the late 17th century. It was originally a residence thought to have been built by one George Hawes whose family estate was Caldmore. It became an inn sometime around 1818 and was known as Ye Olde White Hart. The building has found lasting fame as the home of the 'Hand of glory' and the 'Caldmore ghost'.

The 'Hand of Glory' was discovered hidden in a chimney during renovation work in the late 1870s. It is a mummified arm which is now on display in Walsall Museum. It was once thought that such arms, torn from hanged corpses, could be used by burglars as a candle by lighting the fingers or else as a candle holder. Anyone seeing the flame would be rendered senseless and would also ensure that no household members would wake up whilst their homes were being robbed. The belief was that the flames could only be extinguished with milk.

It is more likely that this arm, which came from a child, was actually a medical specimen. This was supported by the University of Birmingham in the 1960s who confirmed that far from being torn off a corpse the arm had been very skilfully dissected.

Nevertheless, since the discovery there were numerous stories of a child's hand print appearing in the dust and inexplicable banging. A child is said to haunt the building no doubt searching for the arm which is no longer there.

Walsall Manor Hospital
Moat Road
Walsall
WS2 9PS

52.583053, -1.995944

Parts of Walsall Manor Hospital date back to 1838 and the building of the Walsall Union Workhouse. Over the years buildings were added and updated to create the hospital it is today. The original Guardians' building is the only remaining clue to the site's poor law origins as a workhouse and infirmary.

There are a number of ghostly stories from Walsall Manor but two in particular have endured over the years. The first is of an old nun who has been seen on the wards in the east wing particularly by staff. Although she has on occasions frightened the night nurses who have witnessed her, there is nothing to suggest that she is anything but a benign presence.

The second ghost is that of a nurse in old fashioned uniform who again walks the wards. However, she does not walk on the floor as it is today. Apparently, in earlier times when a workhouse infirmary was housed on the site the floors were lower which is why the feet and ankles of the phantom nurse are never seen.

Both of these apparitions have been seen by patients at night and wrongly assumed to be members of staff in spite of their rather strange attire. Nevertheless, these nocturnal visitors are said to be a source of great comfort to the patients they appear to.

Wednesbury

Anchor Hotel
36 Holyhead Road
Wednesbury
WS10 7DF

52.550252, -2.021156

The former Anchor Hotel dates back to 1870 and was also known as the Anchor Inn. At one time a posting house, horses would be stabled here for the use of travellers. The building has been subject to paranormal activity over a great number of years.

The dumb waiter would operate of its own accord even though it was not faulty, dogs would refuse to go upstairs and would bark and growl at things no one else could see. Doors would often get locked or unlocked and open and close by themselves as if some unseen person were passing through. Staff also disliked going down into the cellar on their own.

Since becoming a dance studio, the activity has continued with doors opening and closing on their own when nobody is near. A door to a changing room was found to have been locked whilst the room was in use. There was no explanation for how the door came to be locked and it had to be forced open to release the occupants! The dance academy has a number of framed photographs on display along a particular corridor. Every two to three weeks on average one or more of these photographs would be found smashed on the floor providing regular work for the local picture framer.

Horse and Jockey
Wood Green Road
Wednesbury
WS10 9AX

52.559825, -2.008184

The Horse and Jockey has been operating as a public house on this site since at least 1818. In the 1800s the pub was known as the Old Horse and Jockey. The pub's name may be connected with the racecourse which once existed in nearby Walsall between 1754 and 1876.

The pub features an unusual ceramic bar counter which is connected with a tragic suicide and the subsequent haunting here. The story goes that a man in a long overcoat walked in and approached the bar counter. He ordered a double brandy which he quickly downed in one. Taking out a hand gun from his overcoat pocket the man put it to his head and pulled the trigger, immediately falling dead across the counter.

'Cyril' as he is called now haunts the Horse and Jockey and makes his presence felt in a number of ways. Loud bangs are heard, and cold spots felt particularly in the bar area where he shot himself. Lights get turned on and off, particularly on the back stairs. A man in a long overcoat has been seen in the area of the toilets by both staff and customers. Whilst cleaning early one morning the gentleman's toilet door started banging for no reason. When the cleaner went to look she clearly saw the man in the long overcoat reflected in one of the toilet mirrors. She was alone in the pub at the time.

The same man has been seen by staff coming down the back steps leading from the car park as if to enter the pub. Fully expecting him to come into the bar when they look again there is no-one there. Given the manner of his violent death perhaps this is just as well.

St Bartholomews Church
4 Little Hill
Wednesbury
WS10 9DE

52.555915, -2.020501

Saint Bartholomew's Church is late 15th or early 16th century but thought to be built on the site of a much earlier 13th century church. It was extensively renovated in the Victorian era. The church is known locally as the 'black church' due to the dark weathering of the stonework.

The area around St Bartholomew's Church is associated with Ethelfleda, daughter of Alfred the Great and known as 'The Lady of Mercia'. She is reputed to have created a fortification on the site in the 10th century to provide a defence against the Vikings.

Ethelfleda herself is said to haunt this area around the church and has been seen crossing the gardens and disappearing through a solid wall. Possibly, she is the reported 'Grey Lady' who has also been reported wandering around the churchyard. Rather less likely, she is also seen in the church itself looking out of one of the upper windows. As Ethelfleda predates the church here by some centuries it seems more likely that more than one apparition resides here.

Other buildings in the immediate vicinity also report ghostly activity. In the former Labour Club, the sound of something being dragged across the floor and a woman crying has been heard. A little girl with long blonde hair was seen to walk across the bar after closing time and promptly disappear.

Walkers Bingo Hall
Walsall Street
Wednesbury
WS10 9BY

52.553249, -2.018669

Walker's Bingo Hall opened in 1976 having taken over the old cinema. It was closed at the time of writing. The building dates back to 1915 when it opened as 'The Picture House' showing silent films to packed houses.

The building has long been subject to poltergeist type activity. Things get thrown around and people tapped on the back when there is nobody there.

When the former cinema was being converted into a bingo hall the caretaker at the time took a large delivery of toilet rolls. These were all neatly stacked up but not for long. The toilet rolls ended up being thrown all over the auditorium. This was witnessed by some of the workmen in the building and the caretaker refused to stay in the building on his own.

Anthony Cartwright was employed to do some interior painting during the 1990s. Anthony recalls the following incidents:

Whilst working alone at night I felt what I thought was someone's hand on my shoulder. There was a sudden chill in the immediate area where I was working. I was convinced it was a ghost. I wasn't the only one to have such an experience. Sometime before my scare one of the cleaners was cleaning the toilets when she reportedly saw the reflection of someone in the mirror, she immediately started looking for whoever it was, but soon realised she was alone. she ran from the building, and never went back, not even for her wages.

Ye Olde Leathern Bottle
Vicarage Road
Wednesbury
WS10 9DW

52.557765, -2.011639

Ye Olde Leathern Bottle dates back to the early 16th century and according to local legend was even once visited by Dick Turpin in the 18th century whilst on his way from London to York. The pub plays host to a variety of paranormal activity particularly in the little front snug which was once part of the Vicarage of nearby St Bartholomews.

Staff coming to work in the mornings are sometimes greeted by the strong and unmistakeable smell of toast in the pub even though no one has been in the kitchen. Footsteps are often heard particularly when staff are in the cellar and there is no-one upstairs in the pub. Some of these footsteps sound like a lady in very high heels.

At least three apparitions have been seen in the pub. These include a lady and an old man in grey who do not appear to be associated with each other. The old man in grey is seen in the snug and he appears to resent the presence of ladies in there. If they sit by the old blocked off staircase ladies can expect to feel uncomfortable and experience extreme temperature drops.

Another ghost haunting the snug is connected to a particularly tragic incident in Wednesbury's history. On the 31st January 1916 Kapitänleutnant Max Dietrich, commanding Zeppelin L 21, launched a terrifying raid on Wednesbury killing thirteen people. One of the men killed in the raid was a regular customer at the pub. And it appears he still is.

West Bromwich

Manor House
Hall Green Road
West Bromwich
B71 2EA

52.546678, -1.993119

The Manor House West Bromwich is now preserved by Sandwell Council as a museum and is open to the public. This Grade 1 listed building dates back to the 13th century and retains the original moat and Chapel. The building was used for many years as a pub and restaurant.

There have been numerous reliable reports of paranormal activity in and around the buildings. In the grounds and around the moat hooded figures have been seen resembling monks. An old lady and gentleman have been seen staring out of the upstairs windows by staff after the building has been cleared of visitors and locked up for the night. Apparitions have also been seen in both the Great Hall and the upstairs area known as the Solar bar when the building was used as a pub. On two separate paranormal investigations a shadowy figure was seen briefly in the Solar bar including one sighting by the author. In the Great Hall a long-haired figure was seen wearing a brown jacket. He caught the eye of the investigator present and promptly vanished.

The building is also subject to anomalous light effects. The author and a colleague observed small white lights appearing over some minutes in a tiny panelled room off the Great Hall. Elsewhere similar red lights were observed. No logical explanations for these strange light effects could be discovered.

During one investigation the author could see a dark figure moving around in the Great Hall through some knot holes in an old wooden door. On checking the other side of the door, it was clear no-one had been there.

Sandwell Central Library

316 High Street
West Bromwich
B70 8DZ

52.520368, -1.997476

The magnificent Public Library building in West Bromwich is Grade II listed and established in 1907. A plaque records that, 'This building is the gift of Mr Andrew Carnegie to the Borough' and shows it was one of a large number of libraries across the country financed by businessman and philanthropist Andrew Carnegie. It adjoined an earlier Free Library in the High Street which dated back to the 1870s.

Now known as Sandwell Central Library the building has a long history of paranormal activity. Inexplicable knocks and bangs can often be heard throughout the building and, typical of poltergeist type activity, things get moved around even though nobody has touched them. Objects mysteriously disappear, only to be discovered again usually in a very obvious place.

Strange figures have been seen in some of the rooms including the quite bizarre sighting of a pair of legs striding purposefully across one of the floors!

Sometimes books are found to have been taken off the shelves. Staff can be certain that everything is in place only to later find books have been left out on the tables when no-one has been near. Perhaps the building is still being visited by long deceased borrowers from the past.

Sandwell Hall Gateway
Birmingham Road
West Bromwich
B71 4JS

52.511617, -1.974120

A motorway island seems to be a most odd place to be haunted but nevertheless there are a number of reports of figures seen here. The remains of an old building known as Sandwell Arch can be seen in the centre of the island. This was the gateway entrance to Sandwell Hall built in 1738 and is now Grade II listed. The protected estate of Sandwell Hall was once the seat of the Earls of Dartmouth. The hall itself was demolished in 1928 but much of the estate is now the Sandwell Valley Country Park.

A hooded figure has been seen by both drivers and passengers in this area. The apparition typically crosses the road totally ignoring any traffic before disappearing. Given that the figure is hooded it is likely the apparition is associated with Sandwell Priory, a 12th century Benedictine Monastery, which was situated nearby in what is now Sandwell Valley (see page 136).

The other figure seen around the island is a lady dressed all in white. She is usually seen in the early hours of the morning and is often mistaken for a hitchhiker. Witnesses quickly realise she is no ordinary hitchhiker when they stop to offer her a lift and find she has vanished.

Sandwell Priory
Salter's Lane
West Bromwich
B71 4BG

52.519758, -1.965016

The remains of Sandwell Priory stand in Sandwell Country Park and are accessed through the park. The Priory goes back to the 1100s and Benedictine monks lived and worked there. The Priory ceased to exist except as a ruin after the dissolution of the monasteries under Henry VIII in 1525. However, the estate remained virtually intact and Sandwell Hall was built in the 18th century over the monastery ruins.

Benedictines were known as 'black monks' due their wearing of black habits. There have been many reports of a 'black monk' seen in the general area of the ruins and also around the later Sandwell Hall Gateway (see page 135). The frequency of these various sightings has not gone unnoticed by paranormal research groups over the years and there have been a number of organised investigations here.

Sandwell Valley has a number of pools. Some of these are relatively recent being WWII bomb craters. However, nearby Swan Pool was originally a mill pond and is also known by the older name of Wasson Pool. This pool is said to be haunted. A white, misty shape has been seen to appear some nights hovering over the pool. This apparition floats around above the water and just below the trees until finally disappearing.

The Brittania
Dial Lane
West Bromwich
B70 0EF

52.534309, -2.018250

The original Victorian Brittania Pub opened in 1858 was replaced by a more modern building in 1962 (pictured). This in turn has now become the New Brittania Wedding Venue and Function Hall which opened in 2014.

The paranormal activity here seems to be associated with the earlier pub which was built on the same site. The building is reputed to be haunted by a ghost who has been nicknamed Ebeneezer after a local street. According to bar staff when he is around Ebeneezer is responsible for areas of intense cold and poltergeist type activity. He turns lights on and off and knocks beer glasses off the shelves. He has also been known to turn the cookers on and off in the kitchen.

Ebeneezer has also been known to put in an appearance from time to time. On one occasion a local customer of the earlier pub was paying a visit to the gentleman's toilet when he began to experience the intense cold. This time though it was accompanied by the ghost of a tall man dressed in a long coat and an old-fashioned trilby hat. The apparition then dissolved into thin air right in front of the startled customer.

The New Talbot
41 Black Lake
West Bromwich
B70 0PR

52.533512, -2.009805

Despite the name the New Talbot dates back to at least the 1870s but may be even earlier as it originally held a two guinea beerhouse license following Wellington's 1830 Beer Act. The public house underwent a major refurbishment in 2012 and this seems to have stirred up some paranormal activity in the old building.

Following the renovations, the new manager quickly came to realise that the pub could very well be haunted. After losing his mobile phone in the bar early one morning he decided to check security camera footage to see where it had gone. Part of the footage shows the phone flying off a chair and landing on the floor over three feet away. There was no-one anywhere near the chair or the phone when it flew off.

Strange orb like lights have also been seen on the walls inside the pub and people have been touched on the shoulder when there is no one behind them.

Regulars and staff at the pub put the activity down to a former landlord who died of a heart attack in the pub. One regular customer whose father used to run the pub remembered the deceased landlord very well. Apparently, the seat the phone was thrown from was where he always used to sit.

The Oak House
Oak Road
West Bromwich
B70 8HJ

52.515660, -2.004205

The Oak House Museum in West Bromwich is a fine old timber framed Yeoman's house dating back to the late 16th century. Nobody knows who originally owned the house but by 1634 it was the family home of the Turton family. Nowadays it is run by Sandwell Council as a museum and is open to the public.

A variety of paranormal activity is experienced here by both staff and visitors alike. When the building is quiet a conversation between a man and a woman can sometimes be heard as can singing and children laughing and playing. No amount of searching ever reveals who or where these people are in the building. The children's dressing up clothes can be tidied away only to be found strewn all over the floor immediately afterwards. People have been known to experience physical activity as well in the form of being pushed or prodded when there is no one near.

The kitchen is reputed to be one of the most haunted areas of the house. It is here that an old lady in black has been seen to sit and glare at visitors who come in making them feel most unwelcome. Naturally they assume her to be a member of staff or a volunteer. She is so unpleasant that visitors are often moved to complain about her. They soon discover that no staff members or volunteers dressed in black are based in the kitchen.

The Old Hop Pole
High Street
West Bromwich
B70 9LD

52.523623, -2.002988

The Old Hop Pole in Carters Green is recorded as operating as a public house at least as early as 1867. It originally held a two guinea beerhouse license brought in by Wellington's 1830 Beer Act. The pub has interesting stained-glass panels from the old Showell's Brewery established in 1867 and sold to Samuel Allsopp and Sons Ltd in 1914.

One of the previous landlords had a particularly frightening experience in the cellar here. Things would often go missing and get moved around down there but on this occasion the landlord, who was not a small man, was physically picked up and hurled against the wall by some invisible force.

The Old Hop Pole has a little snug which for some reason seems to be a particular focus for paranormal activity. The apparitions of a little boy and girl in Victorian clothes have been seen here and icy chills can be experienced even when the rest of the pub is warm.

An older gentleman in a cap has also been seen in the snug. On one occasion he was seen by two young ladies together. He is thought to be the ghost of a much earlier landlord who reputedly died in the snug whilst counting up his takings. Another possibility is that he is Alfred Kendrick another former landlord. He met a sudden and unexplained death in the pub in 1885. All this activity did not go unnoticed by a former pub cat. He was known to sit for hours staring intently into the little snug.

Willenhall

Alcatraz Rock Club
Cemetery Road
Willenhall
WV13 1DP

52.588026, -2.054240

The Alcatraz Rock Club was formerly the Ponderosa Club and the building has been shut down for some years now. Willenhall was particularly known as the centre of lock making in the Black Country and the building was most likely a lock factory in earlier times.

The building has been the scene of a great deal of reported paranormal activity. Staff often used to have the feeling of being watched. Tall, shadowy figures were witnessed in the vicinity of the staircase. A man described as being a 'tall, dark, cloaked figure' has been seen more than once in the bar area of the building whilst staff and customers alike have had the experience of being touched or pushed by unseen hands.

Poltergeist type activity has also been reported here with electrical equipment such as light switches being interfered with. Perhaps most startling of all chairs have been known to move across the floor even whilst customers have been sitting on them!

A girl in the ladies' toilets had the unnerving experience of feeling her hair being lifted from her face by invisible fingers. Female customers had a good excuse for not going to the loo alone in the Alcatraz.

Dale House & Malthouse
Bilston Street
Willenhall
WV13 2AW

52.583043, -2.054632

Dale House dates back to 1750. Once an impressive town house the building has for some years been used as a restaurant. Wealthy Thomas Hincks (1715 to 1777), a farmer and maltster, lived in Dale House together with his family.

Thomas was a very prominent local citizen and Chapel Warden. His successful malthouse was situated next door. The malthouse eventually became the Coliseum Cinema in 1914 and later the Dale Cinema from 1932. Having spent some time as a bingo hall this building is now a Wetherspoon's public house, rather fittingly called The Malthouse.

In 1827 a feud between the men of Willenhall and the men of Darlaston culminated in the theft of a fine weather cock from the church steeple. As Chapel Warden Thomas Hincks was instrumental in offering a 10 guineas reward for its return. The weather cock was eventually found in an old mine and returned to its former prominent position to taunt the men of Darlaston!

Both buildings are allegedly haunted, and it may well be that there is a connection dating back to the time when the prominent Hincks family were in residence. The presence of an apparition described as a 'gentleman' has been seen mainly in Dale House by restaurant staff but also in the former malthouse next door particularly when it was in use as a cinema. A good candidate for the ghost here is a member of the Hincks family or even Thomas himself, perhaps still keeping a watchful eye on the family's former home and business.

Locksmith's House
New Road
Willenhall
WV13 2DA

52.583297, -2.059065

The Locksmith's House in Willenhall is now part of the Black Country Living Museum. It is typical of the small lock making enterprises which flourished in the area. The building dates to 1840 but the museum celebrates the lives of the Hodson family who took over the house and workshop in 1904. Two apparitions have been seen here but they seem to be from an earlier time.

Late one afternoon a member of staff was locking up and had gone upstairs. From the bedroom, a flight of stairs goes up to what is now a small office. As she approached the stairs two children were making their way down. It was a boy and a girl dressed in Victorian style clothes. They seemed to be completely benign and not at all frightening according to the lady who witnessed them. She watched them descending the stairs together until they 'simply faded away'. They were in view long enough to ascertain that they came from a fairly well to do family judging by the way they were dressed.

A psychic working on one of the Halloween nights visited during the day with his wife and children. Without knowing anything about the two children he was able to pick them up. He said that they didn't have to be here. They didn't live here. They just liked to visit now and again. And perhaps they still do. Very often staff upstairs in the office area will clearly hear someone come in downstairs. When they go to look there is no-one there.

Rough Wood
Hunts Lane
Willenhall
WV12 5NZ

52.605333, -2.029167

Rough Wood was once part of the Bentley Hay district of Cannock Forest. It was a royal hunting forest recorded as far back as the 12th century. The ancient woodland which contains the largest number of oak trees in the Walsall area is now preserved as a nature reserve.

There have been a number of paranormal sightings here including three apparitions generally described as a nun and also someone who committed suicide in the wood. Very little is known about these but the third ghost who is the most well known locally is that of a lady called Pauline Kelly.

Pauline Kelly disappeared and was presumed to have been murdered sometime in the middle 1800s. Her body was rumoured to have been dumped in the nearby lake although there seems to be little evidence that this was the case. Shortly after Pauline's disappearance her baby daughter, Evelyn, was kidnapped and possibly murdered also. Since then, there have been reported sightings of a lady dressed all in white who wanders the woods presumably searching for her lost daughter.

Local tradition has it that her ghost will appear if a somewhat cruel rhyme is chanted, 'White Lady, White Lady, I'm the one who killed your baby'.

Wood Street Cemetery
Wood Street
Willenhall
WV13 1JY

52.586333, -2.051833

Wood Street Cemetery dates back to 1849 and burials took place there right up until 1986. Originally a Wesleyan Methodist cemetery, it became a municipal cemetery in 1857. When burials commenced in Wood Street Cemetery the land was still owned by George Benjamin Thorneycroft until he sold it to the Methodist Church in 1851. George Thorneycroft was the father of Colonel Thomas Thorneycroft who was born in Willenhall (see page 109).

Some quite prominent Willenhall families are buried in the Wood Street Cemetery including members of the Hodson family who owned the Locksmith's House in New Road (see page 143) which is now part of the Black Country Living Museum.

The old chapel here was demolished in the 1960s but one particular room at the back had gained a reputation for being haunted. People entering the room would sometimes experience an intense cold and be enveloped by a feeling of utter dread.

Although the chapel has long gone the old cemetery itself is said to be haunted by a male ghost. He is a tall, dark figure who moves silently around the cemetery. This figure may be connected with the haunting of the chapel as he certainly puts a scare into anyone unfortunate enough to encounter him. Especially when he suddenly looms up from behind the gravestones.

Wollaston

The Unicorn
Bridgnorth Road
Wollaston
DY8 3NX

52.460038, -2.164821

The Unicorn is a very traditional hostelry dating back to 1859. At that time the brewing of beer took place on the premises. Wellington's Beer Act of 1830 had enabled numerous such buildings to be used for the sale of beer after purchasing a two guinea beerhouse licence.

Many people who took out a beerhouse licence had an alternative trade and the earliest listed licensee of the Unicorn was no exception. Joseph Larkin was a foundry mould maker and rather usefully for running a public house in the 1850s, a bare-knuckle fighter. Since 1992 it has been owned by local real ale brewery, Bathams.

The Unicorn has been subject to some quite specific poltergeist type activity over the years. It is mainly customers of the pub who have to bear the brunt of this activity. It is put down to the spirit of a previous landlord who has seemingly remained attached the pub he once ran.

He seems to like nothing better than to tip full pints of beer into the laps of unsuspecting customers. Maybe he is a ghost with a sense of humour or perhaps he is trying to encourage the sale of more Batham's real ale!

Wolverhampton

Atlantis Nightclub
Bilston Street
Wolverhampton
WV1 3AW

52.583936, -2.125102

The building started life as The Savoy Cinema, which opened on 20th December 1937. Later on, in 1960, its name changed to the ABC. Times were changing for big cinemas such as this and despite converting to a small multiscreen in 1974 the cinema finally closed in 1991.

The old cinema reopened as the Atlantis nightclub and has gone through a couple of incarnations since stories that it was haunted emerged in a local newspaper. It eventually became the Oceana nightclub and later Faces although at the time of writing this too had closed. Although the front has been drastically remodelled the original structure of the original cinema remains including the cellar area.

The paranormal activity here seems to have been centred around the older parts of the building. Staff have had some quite unnerving experiences particularly in and around the old cellars. Shadowy figures have been seen flitting around the building particularly after club goers had left in the early hours of the morning.

Glasses would get smashed for no reason and the cellar doors used to open and close of their own accord as if someone was passing through. The sounds of laughter and singing heard in the old cellar did nothing to reassure club staff that it wasn't indeed haunted.

Exchange Vaults
Cheapside
Wolverhampton
WV1 1TS

52.586390, -2.128749

The Exchange Vaults dates back to at least 1866 and was also known as The Exchange Hotel and is now called The Cuban Exchange. In the 1800s The Exchange Vaults had something of a reputation for being the haunt of criminals.

The ghosts that haunt this pub have military connections with both the First and Second World Wars. When Captain Roger Tart of The South Staffordshire Regiment left for the front he told regulars to save his seat in the corner of the bar. He never returned but that corner of the bar is subject to extreme temperature drops and an old photograph which used to hang there was said to change colour from time to time.

During the Second World War a sailor, Andrew Beswick, had an illicit affair with a local married lady. Her husband, a very jealous and violent man, eventually found out and Andrew Beswick's ghost now haunts the pub.

Strange occurrences abound here. Staff get used to having their names called by what sounds like a little girl. Lights flicker, and the cellar is plagued with electrical problems even though the wiring is sound. Bar stools get moved around both in the bar and the cellar.

One member of staff, Darren, was in the cellar on his own changing a barrel and turned around to find a bar stool had been silently placed right behind him and blocking his way out.

Express and Star Building
51-53 Queen Street
Wolverhampton
WV1 1ES

52.585501, -2.124782

The Express and Star building which opened in 1934 is a magnificent Art Deco edifice designed by Wolverhampton architect, Marcus Brown. It was built on the site of a row of much earlier Georgian houses and is now locally listed by Wolverhampton City Council. Built to house the Express and Star, it is still used as the Express and Star Newspaper Group main offices.

There have long been stories that the building is haunted. Unfortunately, there is no real evidence to prove that the event said to be the source of the reported paranormal activity ever happened.

The tragic story associated with the building is that many years ago a young girl accidentally fell down the lift shaft and was killed. Whether this story is genuine or not nevertheless the building has been subject to paranormal activity.

The little girl is said to haunt the building and has been seen by staff working there to manifest as a strange blue mist which appears from nowhere and disappears again just as quickly. A few years back this blue mist was experienced by the night watchman, Kelvin. He was in the Publications Department when the mist appeared in front of him.

Given the lack of any hard evidence for a little girl falling down the lift shaft it may well be that the activity which is experienced here has something to do with the earlier Georgian houses which were on the same site.

Feline and Firkin
Princess Street
Wolverhampton
WV1 1HW

52.586345, -2.125532

The Feline and Firkin is recorded as being a public house as early as 1818. At that time, it was known as The Dog, later to become The Greyhound. Since then, the pub has been known by a variety of names over the years and is now called Billy Wrights. In fact, between 2001 and 2011 when it reopened as Billy Wrights, the pub was almost constantly opening and closing under various names.

The apparitions reported here are rather unusual as ghosts go as they are reputed to be linked with each other. One is a member of Her Majesty's Constabulary. Her Majesty in this case being Queen Victoria of course. He is an old-fashioned policeman in a splendidly ornate uniform. When the Victorian officer is seen it has always been in the area of the main bar. He is said to be looking for the other apparition seen here, a local villain of the same time period known as 'Jack the Hat'. During Victorian times certain areas of Wolverhampton and various notorious public houses and beerhouses were absolutely rife with prostitution and criminal activity of various kinds. Unfortunately, nothing is known of Jack's crimes, but they must have been sufficiently heinous to be pursued even beyond death.

Giffard Arms
Victoria Street
Wolverhampton
WV1 3NX

52.584840, -2.129688

The Grade II listed Giffard Arms on Victoria Street with its Gothic styling looks as though it should be haunted, and indeed it is. The building looks older than it is being only opened in 1929 but replacing a much earlier inn on the same site.

A good deal of paranormal activity is reported at the Giffard Arms. Apart from poltergeist type activity such as glasses moving or exploding and doors slamming on their own there are at least three apparitions documented here.

Two of the ghosts may be experienced in the bar. A little girl has been seen playing here and a long dead landlord called John still likes to check that the pub is secure at night as he strides purposefully through the bar. Indeed, he passes right through the current bar as it didn't exist in his time.

The other ghost associated with the Giffard Arms is that of Anne Horton. She was a prostitute who appears to have lingered from a time before the present pub was built. She is said to have eventually committed suicide in the building. It seems she had a tendency to give her favours away if she took a liking to any young gentleman. Indeed, her ghost has been known to follow young men home if she particularly takes a fancy to them!

Grand Theatre
Lichfield Street
Wolverhampton
WV1 1DE

52.586593, -2.124179

The Grand Theatre first opened its doors in 1894 and still retains it magnificent Victorian facade. The theatre has played host to many glittering stars over the years including a young Charlie Chaplin in 1902 who, according to recent evidence, may well have been born locally in Smethwick at what is now Black Patch Park (see page 94).

In common with many other theatres The Grand in Wolverhampton is allegedly haunted by at least two ghosts. The most well-known apparition here is one Mr Percy Purdy. He was the manager for some years in the early part of the 20th century and still likes to keep an eye on productions. He has been seen on numerous occasions including by one of the cleaners in the auditorium. As she looked at the immaculately dressed gentleman he simply vanished away in front of her. He has been seen at the end of the day making his way to the old downstairs bar where he liked to pour himself a whisky.

The second reported ghost at The Grand is not actually seen but makes her presence felt through the strong smell of lavender perfume and a distinct chill. She is sometimes known as the 'Lavender Lady'. This lady is often experienced around the stage area where the story goes that she was killed in a fall. Stories vary as to who she was and how she came to fall. In one version she fell from the stage and in another from one of the boxes above.

Mr Purdy is also reputed to be responsible for breaking glasses in the bar area. This seems a little unlikely given his obvious love of the building so perhaps there is a third entity who is a bit more mischievous?

Hog's Head
Stafford Street
Wolverhampton
WV1 1NA

52.587333, -2.125816

The Hog's Head, dating back to the early 1800s, used to be known as The Vine and The Vine Hotel. The pub had a rather unusual resurrection as in 1884 the building was converted into offices. This usually spells the death knell for a pub but not here as it was turned back into the Hog's Head pub in 1998.

As far as is known there are two ghosts here. Back when it was The Vine Hotel in the 1930s, there was a fatal accident in the cellar. The owner at the time had gone down to make some repairs. Carrying some heavy tools, he missed his footing on the steep cellar steps and fell to his death. To this day, his ghost wanders the cellar vainly trying to complete the job he started in life. Staff often feel as though they are being watched in the cellars and are particularly uneasy on the steps where the accident happened.

The other ghost here was a regular customer during World War Two. He is a train driver called Marber. Driving trains was a reserved occupation and so he would not have been called up to fight. Nevertheless, it was a dangerous job in those days and Marber was killed in a bombing raid. If you visit here, look out for the ghost of Marber. He is apt to sit by the bar quietly on his own before suddenly disappearing.

Kings House
St Johns Square
Wolverhampton
WV2 4DT

52.581333, -2.127167

Kings House is a late 18th or early 19th century building. It is now used as an office suite and business centre, but the building was originally part of St Joseph's Convent of the Sisters of Mercy. The convent included the Calvary Chapel, Regents Court, St John's Cloisters and Hanover House. The Convent had the Our Lady of Mercy School attached to it. This school was demolished in the late 1970s, but the original convent buildings now form the modern, internally refurbished offices.

The haunting of King's House appears to have more to do with the associated former school and the Sisters of Mercy who ran it. Stories of the old school being haunted persisted right through from the 1950s and up until the 1970s when the school was finally demolished. Pupils transferred to St Chad's Boys College in Fallings Park which was renamed Our Lady and St Chad.

The apparition seen in the old school is described as being a small nun carrying a lamp. She was reported as being seen during the 1950s by a small group of people in the school. During the 1970s the haunting activity appears to have reached something of a peak. So much so, the part of the school containing the rooms where the nun would regularly walk were locked up and no longer used.

Madame Clarkes
4 - 5 king street
Wolverhampton
WV1 1ST

52.585845, -2.126606

Madame Clarke's Coffee Bar and Restaurant is a splendid Georgian Grade II listed building with an interesting past. Originating in the 18th century the present building is mainly 19th century. It ran ostensibly as a drinking establishment but was also well known as a house of ill repute presided over by Madame Clarke herself.

There are stories of secret tunnels here used by gentlemen who didn't want to be seen, especially by their wives no doubt, entering or leaving by the front door. One such tunnel was said to lead to the Old Still further up the street which itself is haunted (see page 159).

Ladies of the night who frequented the house were known to chalk prices on the soles of their shoes. Should the authorities turn up unexpectedly the charges could easily be erased by simply wiping their feet on the floor!

The building is reputed to be haunted by Madame Clarke herself and indeed she may be the 'grey lady' who has been seen in the property. The sounds of footsteps and inexplicable loud bangs are heard in the building together with disembodied voices. Staff also report that they often have the feeling of being closely watched. Waitresses have even been known to have their bottoms pinched on occasions. Perhaps Madame Clarkes is also haunted by one or more of her errant customers.

Merridale Cemetery
56 Jeffcock Road
Wolverhampton
WV3 7AE

52.579242, -2.150553

Following up a report of an intruder in one of the buildings late one night a Panda car was despatched to Merridale Cemetery to investigate. The key holder had already been contacted by the desk sergeant and the police officer sat in his car to wait.

He didn't have to wait very long. It was raining heavily at the time and after a few minutes an old lady appeared along the street to let him in. They entered the building together and after a check round it is clear everything is secure. They came out and the old lady locked up and went on her way.

The policeman spent a few minutes in his car writing up the incident and was suddenly disturbed by a tap on the window. The man standing there said he was the key holder and had come to open up. The officer explained he had already been in and checked but the man was adamant he was the only key holder.

On entering the building again there was just one set of wet footprints on the floor. The description of the old lady did however match that of a key holder. Except that she had died many years before.

Moseley Old Hall
Moseley Old Hall Lane
Featherstone
WV10 7HY

52.637432, -2.102281

Moseley Old Hall was one of the places where Charles II hid after the ill-fated battle of Worcester in 1651. He was moved here from Boscobel House (see page 85). The building now belongs to the National Trust and a guided tour gives a fascinating glimpse into this aspect of the English Civil War.

The isolated lane outside Moseley Old Hall is haunted by the ghosts of defeated Scottish soldiers returning home from the battle of Worcester. They have been heard immediately outside the house or their presence sensed as they pass by along the lane.

Moseley Old Hall was a Catholic house and the secret chapel upstairs has a very strange atmosphere at times. Many people have felt icy chills up there and some feel decidedly uneasy until they leave. On occasions, a lady in period dress has been seen in the chapel but there is no clue as to who she is.

One of the volunteer guides witnessed the heavily weighted chains on the clock in the King's room being moved by unseen hands during a regular tour. On the same tour, the door to the nearby Whitgreave's Room opened and closed by itself. Outside, as she stood in the corridor the same tour guide had the unnerving experience of feeling an entity pass straight through her which not surprisingly made her feel quite dizzy!

Northycote Farm
Underhill Lane
Bushbury
WV10 7JF

52.626489, -2.105612

Northycote features a fine Tudor farmhouse and is once again a working farm in the care of Wolverhampton City Council and open to the public. The house was built in the year 1600 and for two hundred years was owned by the Catholic Underhill family.

One story associated with the house is that a comely servant girl was ordered to nearby Moseley Old Hall to 'entertain' Charles II in hiding there after the battle of Worcester. This may have been to appease Charles after he was inadvertently refused shelter at Northycote. She reputedly disappeared on her return journey never to be seen or heard of again. The girl had a secret lover, a young farm worker. Broken hearted, he haunts the farm buildings at Northycote still waiting for his long-lost love to return.

There have been other reported sightings at Northycote. A woman has been seen busily sweeping the floor of the tearoom kitchen before promptly disappearing. A polite gentleman in Victorian style clothes was seen in the mirror to doff his hat to a woman in the ladies' toilet before he too vanished.

The silent apparition of a Cavalier was seen by two stallholders at a Christmas fete to ascend the stable block staircase and pass straight through the wall at the top. A Cavalier has also been seen in the farmyard together with the sounds of non-existent horses. On one occasion, loud footsteps and the sound of someone falling were clearly heard coming from an upstairs room directly above the parlour. The room in question was found to be securely locked with no signs that anyone had been up there.

Old Still Inn
King Street
Wolverhampton
WV1 1ST

52.586082, -2.125778

The Grade II listed Old Still was once a private town house built in the mid-1700s. By 1820 it had become The Old Saracens Head public house. By the late 1800s it had become The Old Still. The pub has a fine theatrical tradition as well as its resident ghosts.

The famous soprano, Dame Maggie Teyte, spent her formative years here and many showbusiness stars have called in for a drink whilst treading the boards at the nearby Grand Theatre which is also haunted (see page 152). It was a favourite watering hole for Les Dawson when he was in town.

Two of the reputed ghosts here met their tragic deaths in the pub. One was a former licensee who hung himself back in the Edwardian era. He makes his presence felt in the bar through cold spots and by moving things around. At times he has been known to pull pictures off the walls.

The other was a young child who was also reputedly died by hanging in the building, possibly by accident whilst playing. At quiet times, this child can be heard sobbing from one of the upstairs rooms.

It is said the pub can take on an almost Dickensian atmosphere at times as if the very fabric of the building itself was haunted in some way. And if you are very lucky you may meet Martha. She sits in the corner of the bar just as she has done since the 1800s.

Prince Albert
Railway Street
Wolverhampton
WV1 1LG

52.586982, -2.122887

The present Prince Albert public house opened in 1900 and replaced a much earlier beerhouse which had the Royal Commercial Hotel situated upstairs. For many years the Prince Albert was a public house on the ground floor and also had a hotel on the upper floors. This was the Royal Hotel and from 1911 had its own separate entrance. Since 1999, the Grade II listed building has undergone extensive internal alterations and a major refurbishment.

It is the former Royal Hotel part of the building which is allegedly haunted by a Miss Williams. Miss Williams was known to wear a man's suit, smoke a pipe and ride a powerful motorcycle. After the First World War Miss Williams had a secret lover by the name of Anna who was a Wren in the Royal Navy.

In order to keep their then illicit liaisons secret, Miss Williams would light a candle in Room 13 as a signal that it was safe for Anna to come and meet her lover. Anna was killed in a tragic accident and following the death of Miss Williams, Room 13 was locked up and no longer used as a bedroom. Too many guests had awoken in the night to see a figure standing silently at the bottom of the bed and a candle flickering in the window.

Seamus O'Donnell's
Princess Street
Wolverhampton
WV1 1HQ

52.585637, -2.125871

The former Seamus O'Donnell's pub used to be known as The Talbot and the building has now become a betting shop. The building was originally the Talbot Commercial Hotel and can be traced back to the late 18th century

There are two ghosts associated with the Talbot, but it seems they have no connection to each other. The first is the rather sad story of Frances Johnson who had a relationship with a married licensee. When he grew tired of her Francis was banned from ever entering the pub again. Apparently, she used to scratch at the door begging to be let in, but the landlord would have none of it. She was cruelly nicknamed 'Scratching Fanny' and it is her ghost who can be sometimes heard still scratching at the door to be let in.

The second ghost is known only as George and he is said to appear only around the 15th February each year in the area which was the gentleman's toilets for the pub. He would make his presence felt by tapping gentlemen on the back and has been described as a jovial chap in the style of Fezziwig, a character from Dickens's classic, 'A Christmas Carol'.

White Hart
Worcester Street
Wolverhampton
WV2 4LQ

52.582308, -2.131099

The present White Hart was rebuilt in 1923 from a previous pub on the site which dated back to at least 1818. The earlier public house had its own version of topless barmaids, except the women here far from pulling pints were pulling no punches.

In the 18th and early 19th centuries women's bare-knuckle boxing matches were extremely popular. As well as fighting each other there were also matches between men and women. These were often bloody bare-knuckle prize fights with gouging and kicking perfectly acceptable before the introduction of the Marquess of Queensbury Rules. But even so, these prize fights had little in common with the sort of brutal, bare knuckle battles taking place in the back yards of Black Country pubs such as the White Hart.

Where the White Hart now stands the earlier pub had quite a reputation for women's bare-knuckle boxing. The boxers here were topless women who would often fight behind the pub just for beer slops if no money had been put up by the mainly rough and ready spectators.

One of these women was a foul mouthed and violent character called Elizabeth Cartwright. It is Elizabeth's ghost who is said to haunt the present day White Hart. She is never seen as far as is known but makes her angry presence felt in the pub by throwing things around and violently shoving people out of her way.

Wolverhampton Central Library
Snow Hill
Wolverhampton
WV1 3AX

52.582998, -2.125226

Wolverhampton Central Library was a free library built to commemorate Queen Victoria's Diamond Jubilee in 1897. A competition was launched to find a suitable architect with the remits that the building must not cost more than £10,000 and it must include a reference to the Diamond Jubilee in the design.

The competition was won by Henry Hare with a fine design in the Free Renaissance style. It was somewhat unfortunate that Queen Victoria had already died when the library finally opened its doors in 1902.

The land purchased in 1897 to build the library was the site of the former Old Royal Theatre on the corner of Cleveland Road and Garrick Street. The Grade II listed library is subject to paranormal activity, but this does not necessarily seem to be linked with the old theatre.

From the activity reported here, it seems that the library may well be haunted by the ghost of a former librarian. Staff experience poltergeist type activity at times. Books get moved from the shelves and replaced on different shelves. Nothing too unusual in a busy library of course except that this has been known to happen when staff are certain that no-one has been anywhere near. Sometimes the staff hear what they can only describe as 'disapproving noises' from close behind them when there is nobody there.

There is a librarian's office upstairs where a ghostly figure of a man has occasionally been seen by the window pacing up and down as if agitated. A former librarian perhaps, harking back to a time when 'Silence Please' was very much the order of the day.

Wolverhampton Civic Hall
North Street
Wolverhampton
WV1 1RD

52.586667, -2.130483

Wolverhampton Civic Hall was constructed in 1938 together with the smaller Wulfrun Hall as a major venue for concerts and performances. An open competition was held in 1934 for architects to submit designs for the new building which was won by Lyons and Israel of Ilford, Essex.

A number of buildings had to be demolished to make way for the new Civic Hall. A document in the Wolverhampton Archives dated 7th August 1935 records buildings earmarked for demolition to make way for the new Civic Hall. One of these buildings was a mortuary which was situated in Mitre Fold just off North Street.

There appears to be no particular reason for any ghostly activity here, no tragic events in the building's history to attribute it to as far as is known, unless possibly connected with the former mortuary of course. Nevertheless, staff and visitors alike have had many strange experiences in this Grade II listed building. Figures and shadows are seen in both halls, mysterious voices are heard, and things get moved around in areas where there is no one present.

People also have the sensation of being tapped on the shoulder as if someone were urgently trying to get their attention. Of course, when they turn around to see who it is there is nobody there.

Wolverhampton Railway Station
Railway Drive
Wolverhampton
WV1 1LE

52.587503, -2.120328

The original Wolverhampton Queen Street Station was opened in 1852 four years after Birmingham New Street Station pictured above. The modern-day Platform 4 at New Street Station has become known as a paranormal hotspot with links to this long history. The two stations unusually share the same ghost, nicknamed Claude. He is a finely dressed Victorian gentleman who seems to travel the line between the two stations. Claude is said to have committed suicide by poisoning himself although it should be noted that accidental poisoning was not uncommon in the Victorian era.

Claude has been seen on Platform 4 at New Street particularly in the early hours of the morning. On occasions, he is accompanied by another suicide, Walter Hartles. Walter shot himself in one of the waiting rooms on Platform 4 where he is sometimes seen sitting to this day. Passengers on Platform 4 often have the distinct feeling of someone close behind them. They turn to look and of course there is no-one there. Claude has even been seen riding on present day trains between the two stations. As recently as 2014 a spate of activity was reported on Virgin trains travelling to Wolverhampton involving what was described as a male presence together with sudden unexplained temperature drops. Witnesses usually assume the gentleman is dressed in Victorian costume for some reason, until he disappears in front of them of course.

Wombourne

Bridgnorth Road
Wombourne
DY3 4LN

52.522593, -2.192098

There are a number of stories associated with this stretch of road and they are most likely related. There have been many reports over the years of phantom horsemen heard riding along this section of road particularly around November time. These reports have become, rightly or wrongly, associated with the reputed ghost of Gideon Grove, a servant escaping from the siege of nearby Holbeche House where the Gunpowder Plotters were finally captured or killed (see page 64).

The story goes that Gideon, who played no part in the plot, was trying to escape back to his home in Trysull when he was hunted down by the Sheriff of Worcester's horsemen and cruelly done to death by having his head held down in the marshy ground until he drowned.

This is alleged to have occurred alongside the present day Bridgnorth Road around the area where the South Staffordshire Railway Walk passes under the road. Many believe locally that it is the pursuing horsemen who have been heard to this day. Whether the connection with Gideon Grove is correct, or whether there even was a Gideon Grove, nevertheless stories of phantom horsemen have been reported by very credible witnesses over a good many years.

The Red Lion
Battlefield Hill
Wombourne
WV5 0JJ

52.535828, -2.178187

The Red Lion is the oldest public House in Wombourne. It has held a licence since the early 1800s but the building itself is very much older. It lies in a dip along the ancient medieval road linking Wolverhampton, Worcester and Chester. The pub had its own well for the brewing of beer and this is now covered by a brick pillar in the lounge.

The ghost of a mysterious lady has haunted the Red Lion for many years. When Frank and Lil Ward moved to the pub in 1963 they were told by older locals that she was a previous landlady who had died falling down the cellar steps, but this is debatable. When Frank and Lil first arrived she was very active, never seen at that time but heard banging the doors around the pub.

In the 1980s the ghost was particularly active. It started off with barmaid, Frances, seeing a figure walk past a window in the pub. The author was present at the time and can confirm Frances's surprise when she saw the figure. The window had outside access at the time and was at least 10 feet from the ground.

Shortly afterwards landlord Lee Thacker briefly saw the apparition of a lady in Victorian style dress sitting in the lounge area. He had the pub blessed by local clergy, but this didn't stop the same spectral lady appearing to staff on the security cameras after hours one night. She was sitting in the exact same seat where Lee had witnessed her previously. When staff went to investigate in the securely locked lounge there was nobody there.

Wordsley

Queens Head
High Street
Wordsley
DY8 5QS

52.482615, -2.162036

The Queens Head has been a licensed house since at least 1854. At that time, it held a two guinea beerhouse licence instituted by Wellington's Beer Act of 1830. This was a licence obtained through the local excise officers and did not require the approval of local Magistrates or the Licensing Bench.

The Queens Head plays host to a rather unusual ghost who engages in poltergeist type activity. People in the bar often report feeling someone brush past them even though when they turn around there is no one there. Pennies placed on the bar are sometimes flicked off by invisible fingers and other objects have been suddenly thrown across the floor. On one occasion a heavy iron pot was launched from the range and crashed to the floor, fortunately without injuring anyone present.

Poltergeist activity such as this is fairly common throughout this book but what makes this ghost particularly unusual and indeed unique is that they have a taste in music. When things used to get a little too active for comfort one of the previous landladies would leave a radio playing in the cellar. This would be sure to calm things down as long as the radio was left tuned to a pop music channel!

Red House Glass Cone
High Street
Wordsley
DY8 4AZ

52.475850, -2.157198

The Red House Glass Cone dates back to the late 1700s and was used by the Stuart Crystal glass manufacturing company up until 1936. Glass manufacturer, Richard Bradley, bought the site in 1780 and was producing window glass there from around 1790. The glass cone stands nearly 100 feet high and is one of only four remaining in the United Kingdom. These days it is open to the public as a museum with glass making demonstrations, craft centre and cafe.

As with other industries in the Black Country during the Industrial Revolution working conditions in the glass industry were hot and dangerous. Accidents, deaths and ill health due to toxic chemicals and fumes were commonplace amongst the men, women and children too who worked 12 hours a day in appalling conditions.

It is no great wonder that echoes of all this misery manifest in the form of paranormal activity in and around the glass cone particularly at night when all should be quiet. This activity has been witnessed by staff locking up at night, but visitors as well report strange experiences such as sudden cold spots. Loud footsteps can be heard walking across empty rooms. Inexplicable bumps and bangs are also heard together with snatches of conversation from long gone workers.

The Old Cat
High Street
Wordsley
DY8 5RT

52.480746, -2.161871

The Grade II listed Old Cat is certainly old and was originally converted from a row of cottages which would have been around at the time of the English Civil War. It is reported as operating as an inn from at least 1812 but may well be much earlier.

The pub is haunted by a Royalist soldier in full attire who has startled staff mainly around the cellar area. One possible connection is that Charles II is said to have stopped off at an inn in Wordsley to partake of beer and bread whilst fleeing from the ill-fated Battle of Worcester in 1651.

There have also been sightings of cavalier figures, a phantom carriage and ghostly riders particularly around the area of Barnett Lane. There may be a connection here with the Gunpowder Plot as Stephen Lyttelton and Robert Wintour allegedly hid in the cellar of Paddock Cottage to escape the Sheriff of Worcester. There is a little row of shops there now, one of which used to be a hardware store. In May 2000, the author attended a paranormal investigation here after reports of poltergeist activity with things being moved around and sightings of a cavalier type apparition. Whilst no apparitions were seen, nevertheless a bunch of keys did start moving for no apparent reason.

Other sightings on Barnett Lane include three ladies who went to see why their security light had come on only to see a man they described as being in 17th century attire not walking, but gliding straight past the window. Then there was the couple who said, 'good evening' to a man dressed as a cavalier who they assumed was on his way to a fancy-dress party, only to watch him disappear straight through a thick hedge.

BIBLIOGRAPHY AND FURTHER SOURCES

Books

Alexander, M., *Haunted Inns* (Muller, 1973).
Arnall, C., *Mysterious Occurrences* (Davies, 2009).
Bell, D., *Ghosts and Legends of Staffordshire* (Countryside, 1994).
Bradford, A., *Haunted Pubs and Hotels of Worcestershire* (Hunt End), 1998).
Bradford, A., The *Haunted Midlands* (Brewin Books 2006).
Bradford, A., *The Haunted Midlands* (Brewin Books, 2006).
Glews, P., *Dudley Through Time* (Amberley Publishing, 2010.
Green, A., *Haunted Inns and Taverns* (Shire, 1995).
Hallam, J., *The Haunted Inns of England* (Wolfe, 1972).
Hawthorne, B., *Black Country and Birmingham Ghost Stories* (Bradwell, (2013).
Homer, A. and Taylor, D., *Beer and Spirits* (Amberley Publishing, 2010).
Homer, A., *A Black Country Miscellany* (Tin Typewriter, 2016).
Homer, A., *Haunted Hostelries of Shropshire* (Amberley Publishing, 2012).
Perrins, A., *Ghosts and Folklore around Barr Beacon* (Perrins, 2001).
Playfair, G. L., *The Haunted Pub Guide* (Harrap, 1985).
Poulton-Smith., A., *Black Country Ghosts* (The History Press, 2010).
Solomon, P., *Haunted Black Country* (The History Press, 2010).

Websites

Andrew Homer – www.andrewhomer.co.uk/
History of Wednesbury – www.thehistoryofwednesbury.wordpress.com/
Hitchmough's Black Country Pubs – www.longpull.co.uk/
Paranormal Database – www.paranormaldatabase.com/
The Lost Pubs Project – www.closedpubs.co.uk/
UK Haunted Locations Database – www.paullee.com/ghosts/ghostgeo/

Printed in Great Britain
by Amazon